Roots of Radicalism in the Yorkshire Dales
Airton Friends Meeting and its Antecedents

by Laurel Phillipson

with contributions by Richard Harland

Q

First Published 2020

© Copyright Laurel Phillipson 2020

Published by Quacks Books, 7 Grape Lane, Petergate, York YO1 7HU

Distributed by the publisher and by

Airton Friends Meeting, Calton Lane, Airton, North Yorkshire BD23 4AE

British Library Cataloguing-in-Publication Data

Laurel Phillipson, 2020

Roots of Radicalism in the Yorkshire Dales

ISBN 978-1-912728-18-3

Printed by offset lithography by Quacks the Printer

Contents

1. Introduction

Following on from Continental developments in the sixteenth century, seventeenth-century English Protestant nonconformity expressed itself in two main streams or tendencies, both of which followed Martin Luther's (1483 – 1546) teaching in emphasizing that divine grace is a gift that cannot be earned by human merit. A Puritan moiety emphasised the need for meticulous religious observances: Bible reading, public and family prayers, frequent sermons, catechisms, strict observance of the Sabbath, and the keeping of many fasts, but few feasts. At the opposite end of a fuzzy continuum of beliefs and practices, were clerics and laity who were equally firmly convinced that the essence of religion is not legalistic regulations, but unmediated response to a personal awareness of divine immanence: what Richard Coore (*circa* 1607 – 1687) epitomised as *God sends his Spirit into the hearts of his People... to lead them into all Truth* (Pickering, 2017 p. 20) and George Fox (1624 – 1691) called *that of God in every man*. The inclination to prize personally received spiritual revelation or enlightenment above legalistic formulation goes under the general title of antinomianism. Its English manifestations have had many, sometimes pejorative, names including: Anabaptist, Crypto-Papist, Dissident, Eatonist, Familist, Grindletonian, Independent, Libertine, Perfectionist, Quaker, Ranter, Seeker, and Separatist. It is with some of the people and events associated with these movements that the present work is concerned.

For an introduction to the underlying theological issues David Como's detailed study (2004) is recommended. He has examined English antinomianism as it developed over a wide geographic area, from Yorkshire to London, and a short time span in the 1620s and 1630s; I have taken the opposite approach by looking closely at an area bounded by Langstrothdale and the River Wharfe on the north and east, by Keighley and Pendle Hill in the south, and extending westwards as far as Giggleswick and Grindleton, focusing most closely on Malhamdale and on the development of Quakerism in the small Pennine village of Airton. This area, which approximately encompasses the ancient wapentakes of Staincliffe East and most of Staincliffe West, was the economic heartland of Craven as enumerated in the Domesday Book of 1086. Skipton, its market town and administrative centre, controlled the Aire Gap between the northern and southern ranges of the Pennines and dominated the ancient Roman highway running westwards from York through Ilkley and on into Lancashire. Malhamdale and Malham Moor are geographically central to the area. Within this limited geographic compass of approximately 400 square miles, a long time frame first looks at some of the predisposing social and economic factors which fostered radical nonconformity in Craven and the Yorkshire Dales and then traces their development over the centuries in the history of Airton Friends Meeting.

This study began as a now-superseded pamphlet (Harland and Phillipson 2007) that was widely distributed as part of a major campaign to raise funds for restoration of the Airton Meeting House. As the structural repairs progressed, traces of the architectural history of the Meeting House and its associated buildings were disclosed. At the same time, research into archival records and relevant publications raised questions and revealed significant information about people and events in the Skipton-Airton area pertinent to the early history of the Quaker movement. Who became local Quakers in the 1650s? Why did George Fox go to Pendle Hill? By what route did he travel from there to Sedbergh? Did Major General Lambert and George Fox meet? How closely were Lambert and his family involved with Quakers? Some of the research into these questions was published in 2017 (Phillipson and Armstrong, *Hidden in Plain Sight, history and architecture of the Airton Meeting House*), but much was too detailed or too tangential to find its way into what was intended as a light, popular work. Where that book focused most closely on the physical building, the present work is more concerned with the people who used it. My own involvement with the Airton Meeting House began in about 1997, not long after I moved from Cambridge to Threshfield, near Grassington in the Yorkshire Dales National Park. This was the beginning of two decades of discussions, work and fundraising that culminated in the reopening of the restored Meeting House, together with its associated grounds and buildings, in 2008-2011. It has also resulted in a better understanding of their unique historical significance.

This present work makes use of notes and jottings assembled over a period of more than 60 years: a few were made by Arthur Raistrick, who passed his notes on to Richard Harland. Some were made by Richard, who was especially interested in the Quaker Yearly and General Meetings held in the Skipton area up to the time of the Restoration of the Monarchy in 1660. His memoranda comprise much of chapter seven. My own research interest is primarily related to the history of the Airton Meeting House, the people who used it, and the probability of contact between early Quakers and Major General Lambert. While I have added some narrative interpretation and a bibliography, this compilation does not pretend to be a comprehensive and fully referenced history. Its organisation is roughly chronological, from a cursory look at some of the sixteenth-century national and local antecedents of Quakerism to the restoration of the Airton Friends Meeting House and Barn in the first decades of the twenty-first century, together with a brief mention of some particularities of architecture and furniture of the Meeting House. It has grown with and out of the work of restoring the Airton Quaker property and reinstating its meeting for worship. Discovering and sharing an awareness of the significant position of Airton Meeting House in the early history of Quakerism has helped to justify the contributions of the hundreds of people who generously gave the support, time, money, advice, ideas, permission and permits that enabled the restoration. Since the Meeting House and Barn were reopened, their use by varied groups and organisations and by the thousands of visitors who stop by to see the historic premises and to spend a little time in quiet reflection in the Meeting House and its walled garden are further justification.

Investigation of the Meeting House's origin and subsequent history make it clear that Quakerism was not so much introduced to the Craven area by outsiders as developed, almost coalesced, *in situ*. Airton Meeting House pre-dates the first appearance of Quakerism. Detailed architectural evidence for the age of the Meeting House is presented in Alison Armstrong's vernacular buildings survey (Phillipson and Armstrong, 2017 pp. 35-51) and is not repeated here. While the exact date of the Meeting House's construction on the foundations of a precursor barn is unknown, physical and structural evidence indicates that this was sometime between 1590 and 1620, most probably close to 1610. This conclusion accords with what is known about the domestic and financial circumstances of the Lambert family, who were the relevant landowners. While the Meeting House was being restored under the supervision of James Innerdale, it was examined closely and repeatedly by him and by the late Brian Foxley RIBA. Both architects had special expertise in the conservation of traditional stone buildings. It was also examined by myself as a professional archaeologist, and subsequently by vernacular buildings specialist Alison Armstrong. Initially, each of us expected to find evidence to support a widely-held assumption that the Meeting House had been a rural barn that was subsequently adapted to serve as a meeting house. We looked for, but could find no evidence to support that supposition. When some of the internal wall-plaster and the wainscot panels were temporarily removed we looked for evidence of a blocked barn door in the north wall facing onto the road; when some of the suspended floorboards were lifted, we looked for evidence of an older cobbled or hard-compacted floor. There were no traces of either of these essential features of an agricultural building. Neither was there evidence of any other features which could be interpreted as indicating that the building's original purpose or subsequent use had been as anything other than a meeting house. The only external entrance the Meeting House has ever had is that which it has now. This doorway in the middle of its south wall, facing the hillslope rather than the road, is just 35 inches wide. For almost the first hundred years of its existence the Meeting House presented to passers-by only a blank stone face. In order to site the entrance in what would more customarily have been the building's back wall, more than 700 cubic feet (20 cubic metres) of stony hillside were cut away and the cutting faced by a four-foot-high stone retaining wall and bench. No farmer or landowner would have put such effort into constructing a barn that could only be accessed by way of a restricted passage with a right-angled bend, running along two sides of the building. The coeval retaining wall with its long, integral bench provides definitive evidence that the building was always intended for use by people, not for housing animals or for the storage of farm produce or implements. That the Meeting House has been mistakenly described as a repurposed barn demonstrates how well its builders and original users achieved their intention of concealing its actual function.

As is discussed in chapter four, Quaker meetings were held regularly in Airton in the 1650s, possibly starting as early as 1653. Unless an unwarranted thesis is entertained that there were multiple dissenter congregations in the very small village of Airton and that some group other than Quakers was using the Airton Meeting House, it must be concluded that by the mid-1650s it was a Quaker place of worship. As well as being the earliest extant Quaker meeting house, it may also be the oldest surviving nonconformist or dissenter place of worship in England, and possibly in all of Britain. Circumstantial evidence, which requires corroboration by future research, suggests that before 1652 or 1653 it may have been a central meeting place for a rather nebulous and little-known group called Seekers. Airton Meeting House and its associated burial ground are on land that continued to be owned by Major General Lambert and his family until 1700, when its lease was purchased by William and Alice Ellis, who endowed it to Quaker Trustees in 1706.

Various approaches may be taken when consulting historical evidence and records such as those on which this compilation relies: a limited range of written sources can be accepted as definitive, or at the opposite extreme, many different kinds of information including written records, material remains and probabilities of human behaviour can be called upon to produce a more varied and comprehensive picture. The first approach tends to result in a seemingly precise but not necessarily accurate historical narrative that is disproportionately concerned with a few notable individuals and heroic events. The second approach results in a view of history that is more nuanced and potentially more accurate, but may be less precise and must be circumscribed by statements of probability or possibility. Consideration of the dates engraved on the lintels of seventeenth-century buildings can exemplify the two approaches. It is often said that datestones indicate when a house was built; however, when individual buildings are considered more closely it is sometimes found that a particular example refers to the date of a major rebuilding or to some minor alteration of a pre-existing structure. In other instances, it commemorates a wedding or, as at the Airton Meeting House, a change of ownership. Unless corroborated by additional evidence, datestones do not necessarily designate a building's true age. Similar caveats apply to all forms of written and material records, any of which may have been subject to accidental or deliberate errors and misinterpretations. Because I prefer nuanced accuracy over simplistic precision, the pages that follow are littered with statements of probability, for which no apology is made.

In order to set the scene for what follows, it may be useful to review some critical dates in English history. By an Act of Supremacy in 1536, Henry VIII made himself head of the Church in England and outlawed Roman Catholicism. This was followed by the abolition of monasteries, nunneries and related institutions between 1536 and 1541, when their land and possessions were confiscated by the Crown. An initial Act abolishing chantries and most rural chapels in 1545 was not stringently enforced until the passing of a second Chantries Act by Edward VI in 1548. The short reign of Queen Mary from 1553 to 1558 allowed a respite for traditionally-minded Catholic parishioners and clergy and for some early dissenters. However, during the second half of the sixteenth century, several increasingly stringent Acts imposing conformity to a reformed national church resulted in somewhat arbitrary, but legally crucial, distinctions between Catholic Recusants, Conformists to the Church of England, and Nonconformists. The Pilgrimage of Grace in 1536 – 1537 and the Rising of the North in 1569 were attempts to restore the Roman Catholic church. Outbreak of the Civil War in 1642 and disestablishment of the Church of England in 1646 allowed a variety of ideas, sects and preachers to flourish until 1660, when the Monarchy was restored. Under Charles II, between 1661 and 1665, a series of Acts known as the Clarendon Code instituted increasingly harsh penalties to enforce church attendance, conformity to the Established Church and use of the Book of Common Prayer. A new Act of Supremacy and an Act of Uniformity which came into effect in 1662 again outlawed Roman Catholicism and all nonconformity. Ten years later, in 1672, the Clarendon Code was repealed and a Declaration of Licence temporarily permitted the establishment of some dissenter meeting places, but the Test Act of 1673 and resumption of the Clarendon Code from 1683 to 1685 reimposed penalties for the practices of Roman Catholicism and religious dissent. In 1686, James II issued a new Declaration of Indulgence and, in 1689, Parliament passed the Act of Toleration which permitted nonconformist worship in licensed meeting places.

Relating to the events and people which impinged on Quaker origins and the history of the Airton Meeting House, there are several studies which have yet to be fully researched and written. Foremost among these is a comprehensive, detailed history of the crucial first decades of Quakerism, up to 1660, before the Restoration of the Monarchy and the removal of Friends' central administration from the north of England to London. Two other works which it would be useful and a pleasure to read, if only someone would research and write them, are a full, modern biography of Major General Lambert, and a history of the Seeker community and its relationship to Quakerism. When these several studies come to be written, the Airton Meeting House will figure in each of them. One of several reasons for putting the present compilation on record is the hope that it may be of some use, inspiration, or provocation to future researchers on these and related topics.

In concluding this introduction, I would like to record my grateful thanks to all who have cared for the Airton Meeting House and have been interested in learning about its history and its antecedents. My especial thanks go to my husband, David, for his support and for his help with copy-editing. I am also indebted to Mike Slater, Oliver Pickering, and Tacye Phillipson for their helpful comments on earlier drafts of this manuscript.

2.   Antecedents

Among the many roots and antecedents of Quakerism, three may be singled out as particularly significant in our area: the opposition of landed gentry to attempted extensions of royal prerogative, the resistance of people *of the middling sorts* to the intellectual and financial impositions of absentee priests and tithe-farmers, and the catalytic preaching of George Fox and his associates. At least the first two of these factors had their own antecedents in the mid-sixteenth century. If they were not a direct outcome of the social and economic turmoil resulting from a century of population and price increases, they were undoubtedly affected by it. In 1640, the general level of prices was more than three times that of 1540 (Jennings and the Pateley Bridge Tutorial Class, 1967 p. 121). Although such a rate of inflation may not seem momentous by present-day standards, it would have contributed to a general sense of social and economic insecurity, the more so since it was compounded by wholesale changes in land ownership, with new owners seeking rapid profits through speculation and the enclosure of common lands. While many of the unenfranchised masses starved, some individuals profited from the fluid economic and social conditions of the early seventeenth century. With the dissolution of the monasteries, immense land holdings had been distributed, redistributed, divided and sub-divided to enrich new families of landed gentry including the ancestors of Major General Lambert, and soon thereafter a rising class of independent yeomen farmers, crafts workers and trades people. By the late-sixteenth and early-seventeenth centuries, numerous stone-built barns, field walls and houses replaced earlier, less substantial structures. While some of the lead from abbey roofs become Civil War bullets, it was also made into the pewter tankards and trenchers that replaced their wooden precursors on the dressers of farmhouse kitchens.

Although George Fox (1624 – 1691) and his early associates are often referred to in Quaker histories as *the First Publishers of Truth*, they neither invented nor discovered the religious attitudes, testimonies and practices with which they and the Religious Society of Friends, to give it its formal title, are associated. Their individual and collective energy, preaching abilities, organisational skills and determined persistence served to attract and give expression to ideas which were already deeply embedded and widely held in the Yorkshire and Lancashire countryside. Historical origins can rarely be traced to their ultimate beginnings; each root that one seeks to disentangle is found to have its own multiple antecedents. Perhaps the ideas and understandings that have contributed to present-day Quakerism should be traced back to the fourteenth century when followers of John Wycliffe translated the Bible into English, or to the spread of literacy and the Protestant reformation in the early sixteenth century. Certainly the abolition of press censorship in England in 1642 was a significant factor.

In writing about what may have been the largest and most conspicuous popular political movement of the English Civil War period, Brailsford (1983) says that the Levellers, led by John Lilburne (1614 – 1657), were much influenced by the Anabaptists, founded by Menno Simons (1496 – 1561), who combined a religious expression of the social ideas advocated in More's *Utopia* with a strong sense of corporate identity and discipline. As early as 1524, Anabaptists such as Hans Denck were preaching that the Word of God was present in every individual at all times and in all places (Lowther, 2003 p. 55; Jones, 1914 pp. 17-30). Many of the Levellers, who comprised some of the most active supporters of civic and social reform during the Civil War period, were Anabaptists and some of the earliest Quakers had been Levellers. The breadth of their liberal way of thinking, their numerical strength and their unity of religious and political understanding are embodied in the opening sentence of a petition to Parliament signed by ten thousand Leveller women in 1649: *Since we are assured of our creation in the image of God, of an interest in Christ equal unto men, as also of a proportionate share in the freedoms of the commonwealth...* (Brailsford, 1983 p. 317). The Levellers, who initially formed a major component of the New Model Army, attempted to give their understanding of the equal worth of all a political embodiment by circulating and signing numerous petitions calling for a new form of government based on the consent of the governed. Repeated drafts of a proposed *Agreement of the People* were issued by members of the New Model Army and their elected leaders, or *Agitators*, and by Leveller committees and individuals. These called for a wide franchise, equality of all under the law, the abolition of class privilege, and religious toleration. Attempting to constrain the rising demands coming from below, less liberal editions of this *Agreement* were produced by senior officers of the Army.

In all this, Major General Lambert took a moderate position. He seems genuinely to have wanted a large measure of religious toleration, but even more than toleration, he wanted to maintain stability and peace in the country. When he composed an *Instrument of Government* for the Commonwealth, Lambert took much of its wording from various draft *Agreements of the People* while attempting to steer a course between the wide liberties demanded by the Levellers and their supporters and the restricted liberties which were all that the propertied classes were willing to grant to their fellow countrymen. This *Instrument* and the *Agreements* which preceded it found their most enduring embodiment in the *Constitution* of the United States of America and in the words of its *Declaration of Independence*: *We hold these Truths to be self-evident, that all men are created equal and that they are endowed by their Creator with certain inalienable rights ....* Before the Restoration, this optimistic, socially radical world view was widely expressed, including in Quaker writings. During the final years of the Commonwealth and even more so during the Restoration, the Leveller movement was extinguished. Both among the Anabaptists and the Levellers, who were frequently the same people in their Sunday and in their weekday guises, many who retained a tolerant, democratic, faith-oriented world view gravitated to the Quakers, giving this new movement much of the energy, commitment and excitement which it manifested during its formative years.

A significant factor in the early development of Quakerism was the rise of a large class of people described by some of their contemporaries as being *of the middling sorts*, independent craftsmen, yeoman farmers and others who could support themselves without being closely tied to overlords, and who had learned to read and think for themselves. In the swirl of opinion and counter opinion that characterised the period from the mid-sixteenth to the late-seventeenth century, a welter of sects and theologies was formulated, reflecting their needs and enthusiasms. West Yorkshire and the Craven area were particularly famous, or infamous depending on one's point of view, for the staunchly held independence of religious and political thought in many of its communities. The rapid early adoption and spread of Quakerism in Malhamdale, in Upper Wharfedale, and around Skipton suggests that in the early- to mid-seventeenth century these areas supported many people of independent thought who were attracted by the simplicity and directness of Quaker faith and practice. Others, like Major General Lambert, acknowledged no strongly-held religious affiliation. What might be termed the outlook of the first half of the seventeenth century was much influenced by the so-called new learning, which privileged observation above traditional authority as the source of true knowledge. Transposing this concept from the realms of material science to those of religion and psychology, acceptance of the paramount validity of one's own direct experience was embraced by George Fox and by many early Quakers with all the enthusiasm of a new discovery.

The factors mentioned above were pertinent to a geographic and economic region centred on the Yorkshire Pennines, Craven, adjacent parts of Westmorland, and parts of what is now Lancashire, but was then the West Riding of Yorkshire; they were especially pertinent to our more circumscribed area centred on Malhamdale, Malham Moor and the market town of Skipton. The roots of this distinctiveness can be traced to earlier times. In the twelfth century, large areas of these sparsely-inhabited borderlands were bequeathed or sold to the abbeys, in our area to Fountains Abbey and to Bolton Priory, without coming under the effective control of Norman/English nobility. Initially, the uplands were managed directly by lay brothers and hired labourers for sheep-rearing. Lower areas around Skipton, Embsay, Eastby, in Wharfedale, and in Malhamdale were farmed by tenants who paid feudal dues, rents and tithes. For almost two hundred years the social and economic system appears to have been comfortably stable, until the start of the so-called Little Ice Age when multiple disasters struck (Whyte, 2013. p56). Poor harvests in 1308 to 1310 were followed by markedly cold weather; 1315 was known as the year with no summer and 1316 as the year when it never stopped raining. The resultant failed harvests and sodden fields resulted in massive starvation and disease among people and animals. The numbers of livestock may have declined by almost four-fifths, while human survivors were left unable to resist Scottish raids which took place in 1318 and 1319, and then continued almost annually until 1327 (Butlin, 2003 p.88). In these raids, which were little opposed by English forces, very large parties of mounted raiders advanced down the Vale of York as far as Pickering, then turned westwards along the River Wharfe and through the Aire Gap. In their raids, they had a deliberate policy of killing, burning or destroying whatever they could not carry off in the way of cattle, slaves, crops, metal ware and household goods. Among the villages affected by the raids were: Arncliffe, Carleton, Embsay, Giggleswick, Gisburn, Grassington, Guisley, Ilkley, Kettlewell, Kirkby Malham, Linton, Malham, Settle, and Skipton.

The resultant severe decline in human and animal population destroyed the feudal economy, as there was no longer sufficient labour to maintain the farms. In Kirkby Malham, the tax valuation was reduced by more than fifty percent (Lunnon, 2019 p. 44 fn. 79). Spence (2013, p. 21) says that up to two-thirds of the population of Malham village may have perished. Closer to Bolton Priory, the depopulation was almost total. With no income of farm dues and produce, the Priory was forced to close while its monks were temporarily dispersed and administrators reorganised its systems of land management. Much of the Priory's upland estate was parcelled out to rent-paying tenant farmers, with about a dozen such transactions recorded for Malhamdale and Malham Moor in 1322 (Lunnon, 2019 p. 44). Ending the feudal system transferred the risks and profits of farming and stock-rearing from the Priory to its tenant farmers and to their sub-tenants, enabling people to become more self-reliant and socially self-confident. As repeated plagues affected people and livestock throughout England and Europe in the fourteenth century, death and the after-life became a present concern for many. Although the Black Death of 1348 and its subsequent recurrences affected townspeople and cities more than the countryside, it did have local repercussions. In wealthier parts of England, people endowed chantry altars with redundancies of church plate and jewelled relics which later attracted the attention of Henry VIII and his ministers. In our area, where parishes were large and churches remote, several communities constructed their own rural chapels, to which they appointed priests whom they supported with modest gifts and endowments.

Most of West Yorkshire remained as rural and almost as socially conservative in the fifteenth and sixteenth centuries as it had been throughout the late medieval period, without resident nobility and remote from national centres of power and influence. Especially in our area people were closely interknit by ties of kinship and by the economics of agriculture, wool and weaving, with a large proportion of the population continuing to depend on the monasteries for their farm tenancies or their employment. The social and economic impacts of the dissolution of the monasteries (1536 – 1541), the Chantries Acts (1545 and 1547), the Act of Uniformity (1559), and the Thirty-Nine Articles (1563), all of which destroyed the old basis of religious and social life and sought to institute by decree new ways of thinking, were almost devastating. This is attested by the facts that very many of the approximately 40,000 people involved in the Pilgrimage of Grace in 1536 and most of those involved in the Rising of the North in 1569 were from the Craven area. Most of the destroyed chapels, such as one in Malham dedicated to St Helen and a less-well-known chapel of the same dedication in Airton, had been built and were supported by the ancestors, relatives and neighbours of the people who protested at their destruction (Spence 2015, 2017). Other chapels close to Airton had been in Halton Gill, Hanlith, Hellifield, Hubberholme, Flasby, Settle, and Winterburn.

Harsh penalties inflicted after the non-violent Rising of the North included condemnation to death of one in ten of all its participants. Although most of the so-called rebels were later reprieved, William Lawson of Kirkby Malham was forced to publicly hang his neighbour, William Serjeantson (Spence 2016, 2017). Discontent was also fuelled by the economic consequences of the Henrician (or Cromwellian) reforms. Previously, the monastic houses had supplied a modest level of rural employment, poor-relief and medical care; some parish and chapel priests had served as scribes and school teachers. Little of this was replaced. After a period in crown ownership and large grants to court favourites, much of the land confiscated from the monasteries was subdivided and sold to a new class of profit-seeking landowners whose principal concerns were to maximise their immediate income and who had little respect for traditional tenancies. Several of the relatively few northerners who actively supported the Henrician church reforms, as did the grandfather of the future Major General Lambert, were able to acquire substantial landed estates. These events following hard on the removal of monastic overlordship would have caused many people to turn to the, mostly religiously conservative, local gentry for leadership and others to question more fundamentally the basis of religious belief and worship. Both happened to a marked degree in the Craven area. According to Loughlin (2016, p. 186), *the Reformation was deeply unpopular in the North of England. The Pilgrimage of Grace substantiates this only too well. The Henrician religious innovations – constantly subject to change – were not well received in other parts of the realm...* [but] *opposition was more deeply entrenched in the North... as a result of it being a peripheral region, far removed from the core – the Court.*

Approximately 700, mostly locally-born, monks and nuns were expelled from the monastic houses in Yorkshire (Butlin, 2003 p. 108); a greater number of lay brothers, agents, pensioners and employees must also have been deprived of their livings. As these people were reintegrated into the surrounding communities, they would have strengthened people's resolve to maintain their traditional religious observances. In the second half of the sixteenth century, what had begun as popular religious conservativism evolved into well-defined and growing Catholic Recusancy, quietly supported by influential families of the long-established land-owners and minor gentry, including those of Christopher Marton of Eshton, Richard Whitefield and Thomas Proctor of Winterburn, and John Proctor of Bordley. Although the Pilgrimage of Grace and subsequent disturbances failed in their primary aim of reinstating Roman Catholicism, they seem, for a time, to have impressed the Established Church and State authorities with the overriding need to maintain law and order, even to the extent of not suppressing Recusancy among leading families. Later, towards the end of the sixteenth century, in order to counteract a growing Catholic influence, young, enthusiastic, university-educated Protestant preachers were installed in Craven churches or licensed as itinerant preachers. Among the most influential of these were Christopher Shute, who was in Giggleswick from 1575 to 1626, and Anthony Horrocks, in Kildwick from 1572 to 1588. Others included Edward Horseman in Skipton, Thomas Brodgen, appointed to Burnsall, Adam Rose in Gargrave, Giles Wigginton in Sedbergh, Richard Patchet in Keighley, and Nicholas Walton in Kirkby Malham (Spence 2016). Walton was the local parish priest and schoolmaster when the future Major General John Lambert was a young boy growing up in Calton (Farr 2000). A Cambridge graduate, Robert More, was appointed chaplain to the Countess of Cumberland at Skipton Castle. More was a former pupil of Giggleswick School, where he had been influenced by Shute. He preached widely in Craven, spent a short while in Kildwick parish, became vicar of Guiseley in 1581, and was a loyal supporter of Roger Brearley (1586 – 1637), who is further discussed below. Although these newly-introduced Protestant preachers remained within the Established Church, they tended to be radically inclined, opposing what they saw as retained vestiges of Roman Catholicism in church ritual and vestments.

Both among the clergy and the laity, many began to travel to hear new ideas and eloquent preaching and to attend religious debates and conferences. In 1619, it was recorded of Giggleswick parishioners that *many go to Grindleton and neglect their own parish church* (Spence 2012). Resulting from a Church Visitation in June 1615, Richard Tennant, *son of Henry Tennant of Waterhouses on Malham Moor*, Thomas Armistead, Nicholas Waddington and Roger Brearley were charged with unauthorised preaching in Gisburn parish church. The gentleman farmer Henry Tennant was probably related to the Langstrothdale Tennants who were prominent Quakers in the second half of the seventeenth century; Waterhouses is close to Malham Tarn, about six miles from Airton. Henry Hoyle, the then vicar of Gisburn, was a comfortably well-to-do Nonconformist who held multiple livings. Tennant (born 1591) was Cambridge educated; in May 1619, he married Hoyle's daughter, Mary, and in 1652 Hoyle presented Tennant to the vicarage of Kettlewell. William Boyes, Brearley and Tennant were cited again in 1627 on suspicion of doctrinal heterodoxy (Como, 2004 p. 271). Brearley was charged with unlicensed preaching in Grindleton Chapel and with heretical ideas: that he believed in divine inspiration, preached that a Christian may have God within himself, and that crosses and clerical dress prevented the revelation of God to preacher and to people. Brearley, who was much influenced by the antinomian teaching of a Dutch theologian, Hendrick Niclaes [or Nicholis] (*circa* 1501 – *circa* 1580), was the principal leader of the Grindletonians. He and his followers were named after the town of Grindleton, near Clitheroe. Although Brearley remained within the Established Church, some of the preachers influenced by him described themselves as Independents; they observed a very simple form of worship, trusted the direct inspiration of God's spirit, and did not restrict preaching and prayer to an anointed clergy. During the second quarter of the seventeenth century, clergy in Burnsall, Carleton, and Kildwick advocated the practice of a priestless and sacrament-free religion that resembled or was allied to Grindletonianism. In 1635, the curate of Kildwick, John Webster (1611 – 1682), was charged with being a Grindletonian. He continued to be active in the Pendle area into the 1650s. A preaching exercise in Bingley in 1651 was dominated by antinomians (Pickering, 2017 p. 10).

The Grindletonian movement persisted into the 1680s, most noticeably around Gisburn and Kildwick. Some of its later adherents, probably including Sarah Grimshaw, the daughter of Josiah Collier (1595 - 1677), who was one of Brearley's most active followers, and Thomas Barcroft, a gentleman cloth merchant of Colne, became Quakers. In 1656,

Barcroft circulated a letter urging other Grindletonians to become Quakers. Among the more influential early Quakers who may have had Grindletonian attachments were John Chapman and Francis Howgill. Boyes, who had been one of Brearley's first disciples, subsequently became a Quaker and accompanied Richard Farnsworth on a preaching tour of southern Yorkshire. I have found no evidence that James Nayler, whose family home was about 50 miles from Grindleton, had any affiliation with these people. Nonetheless, it seems most likely that he would have been well aware of and influenced by the ideas of Brearley and Webster. In *Blown by the Spirit*, Como identifies Grindletonianism as a very significant ideological precursor of Quakerism (Como, 2004 pp. 315, 324).

A poorly-documented movement that was influential in the Craven area and in the early formation of Quakerism was supported by a large, but perhaps somewhat loosely affiliated, group of people known as the Seekers. They were anti-clerical, non-Calvinist, anti-Trinitarian Christians who rejected all existing churches, rituals and creeds as corrupt. Instead, they met in silent assemblies where they waited for God to send them a new apostle who would show them a better way of worship and would establish a new church. It is debatable whether in the early seventeenth century the designations Grindletonian and Seeker referred to different persuasions, or whether these were alternative designations for somewhat nebulous groups of liberal-minded people close to the fringe of Protestant thought. Perhaps the two terms referred to different positions along a continuum, with the Grindletonians at least initially willing to remain within the Established Church while trying to reform it from within, while the Seekers withdrew into their own form of largely silent worship. It is to be regretted that relatively little is known about them and there is no comprehensive study of the Seeker movement, only brief hints and the polemical writings of a few seventeenth-century authors. That the Seekers may have been deliberately and successfully clandestine is not implausible. The Dutch leader of the Family of Love, Hendrick Niclaes, had many followers in England; his writings were influential and widely circulated and some were translated into English by Roger Brearley. Niclaes had ties to our area through his business interests in the cloth trade and as a wool merchant. He twice visited England. According to Como (2004 p. 115) Niclaes' *followers were instructed to conform to the customs and regulations of the reigning ecclesiastical power... practising their faith secretly and beyond the institutional boundaries of the visible church. If detected for heresy, dissimulation was not merely permitted but encouraged.* Someone who was perhaps a member of a Seeker congregation was William Sykes of Knottingley near Pontefract. Refusing to pay the then very large fine of £266 13s 4d for testifying against church tithes, he was imprisoned in York Castle, where he died in 1625. The date of his imprisonment gives clear evidence that what was to become a defining Quaker testimony pre-dated the preaching of early Friends.

An author whose writings influenced both Seeker and Quaker thought was the radical preacher, John Saltmarsh (*obit* 1647). He was born in the East Riding, educated at Cambridge University, and served as rector of Heslerton near Malton from about 1637 to 1643. He joined Fairfax's regiment of the New Model Army, where he served as a chaplain. In *Dawnings of Light* (1645) he argued that the present was a time of religious seeking and that all separatist religious groups should be tolerated so long as they contributed to the common good. The following year, in his most widely published work, *Smoke in the Temple*, he argued that the present was a time of waiting because there was then no legitimate church. He proclaimed that the glory that was coming was inward and spiritual. In order to know *Truth*, people must live in the power of *Truth*: *Jesus Christ the Light be in us*. The Seeker rejection of religious compulsion and their confidence in the ultimate and universal redemption of all people probably sheltered a wide range of beliefs; they were known to have strong social and moral concerns. Seekers were particularly numerous in the area around Skipton in the early-

10

seventeenth century. According to Baumber (*circa* 1975), among their most active leaders were Roger Brearley, mentioned above, who was curate of Kildwick church from 1623 to 1629, and John Webster, who was curate of the same church from 1634 to 1643. These two men were also identified by their contemporaries as Grindletonian preachers; the contemporary ascription to either of these movements may have been both nebulous and fluid.

Seeker leaders in the 1640s and early 1650s were the Taylor brothers, Thomas (1617 – 1681) and Christopher (1620 – 1681), who held farmland at Carleton, near Skipton. They had each been educated at Oxford, but soon left the Established Church. Como (2004 p. 322) says that in 1651 Christopher was an antinomian preacher and curate in Halifax, while Thomas was preaching in and around Preston Patrick to a group that included Francis Howgill, John Camm and John Audlin. All five of these men became leading Quakers. Thomas Taylor was a notably energetic and effective preacher and debater (Jones, 2014 p. 220); he is credited with convincing the first Quaker in Countersett, Richard Robinson, that George Fox's teachings opened the way to salvation. George Fox and Thomas Taylor remained in touch with one another; while on his way to Skipton in 1660, Fox stopped to visit Taylor in Carleton. It may have been largely as a result of the Taylor brothers' influence that aspects of the Seekers' organisational structure, including the holding of general and yearly meetings, were adopted by Friends. I have not been able to find any record of where Seekers in our area met after 1643, when John Webster ceased to be curate of Kildwick church, nor of how and where the Taylor brothers exercised their reputed leadership or presidency of the Seekers. Some Seekers meetings could have been held in private houses or, in the summer when they were not used to house hay and cattle, in barns, but larger gatherings would have been too big to hold in private homes and too conspicuous to hold in Skipton or Keighley without notice being taken of their occurrence and some record left. As is discussed in chapter one, above, and elsewhere (Phillipson and Armstrong 2017), Airton Meeting House was purpose-built, most probably in the first decade of the seventeenth century, apparently as a dissenters' meeting place capable of accommodating congregations of one hundred or more people. Circumstantial evidence suggests that it may have been constructed as a place where Seekers could meet under the tacit protection of the Lambert family, on whose land the building stood. If it was from here that Thomas Taylor and his brother exercised their leadership of the Seeker community, this would have made Airton a particularly attractive destination for George Fox on his way from Pendle Hill to Sedbergh in the summer of 1652.

Carleton and Kildwick are small villages located two miles south-west and four miles south of Skipton, with Lower Bradley situated approximately midway between them. As the Watkinson family of Scale House, Rylstone also owned farmland at Lower Bradley, they would have known Roger Brearley, John Webster, and Thomas and Christopher Taylor. The Watkinsons would have been well acquainted with and apparently were sympathetic to Seeker ideas. By 1653, after George Fox's visit to Skipton, and most probably to Airton, in 1652, the Watkinsons were prominent among local Quakers. Gervase Benson, who lived near Sedbergh, was another leading member of the Seekers (Sewel, 1811 p. 88) before he became an influential Friend. He attended Quaker General Meetings in Skipton and Rylstone, and preached to good effect in Airton in 1657 and/or 1658. Members of the Tennant family, who lived at Scarhouse in Langstrothdale and owned property in Skipton, were also Seekers before they joined Friends. When George Fox first visited them in 1652, Scarhouse was already a centre of dissenting Christians. From 1652 or 1653, when the Tennants became Quakers, until their property was sold in 1719, they hosted local meetings and regional gatherings of Friends. A small walled plot at Scarhouse that became a Quaker burial ground was originally a Seeker burial place. While many Seekers joined with George Fox in founding the Quakers, others maintained their Seeker allegiance. It is reputed that large numbers of Seekers attended George Fox's funeral in 1691.

In addition to those who held what were for their time radical religious convictions, there were many others whose radicalism was more political than religious and who supported the Parliamentary army in its attempts to obtain a more democratic form of government. One such family may have been that of Henry Holgate, yeoman. In 1656, he and his wife, Mary, together with their eldest son and his wife, assigned to their younger son, George, a house and three oxgangs of land -- probably 30 acres or more -- in Airton. According to notes made by Richard Harland, several deeds in the Raistrick papers relating to this transaction describe George Holgate as being a Parliamentary soldier in George Watkinson's troop of Col. John Lilburne's Regiment. While Civil War affiliations are known to have split some family loyalties, in this instance the entire family seems to have approved the young man's enlistment sufficiently to agree to settle upon him an inheritance which might otherwise have been withheld until the decease of his parents or denied altogether. John Lilburne was one of the most radical of the New Model Army's political leaders, and it is most likely that George Holgate and through him the rest of his family were exposed to and supported Lilburne's democratic and egalitarian principles. George Watkinson of Scale House, under whom George Holgate served, probably met George Fox in 1652 and was himself a Quaker by 1653. Towards the end of his life, John Lilburne became a Quaker; perhaps George Holgate did likewise, though no Holgate surname is listed among recorded interments in the Airton Friends burial ground. An example of a family with split loyalties is hinted at by an entry in the Kirkby Malham parish register recording the burial in May 1682 of *Anne, daughter of William Atkinson Quaker of Kirkby*. Because they denied the need for and chose to avoid all forms of priestly intervention, Quakers maintained their own records of marriages, deaths and burials and used their own burial plots. Since the earliest recorded burial in the Quaker burial ground in Airton was in 1663, well before Anne Atkinson's death, someone must have made a definite choice not to use it for her interment. While Anne Atkinson may have renounced or moved away from her parents' Quaker faith, other members of her family seem to have remained Friends. Thomas Atkinson of Malham, a possible relative of William and of Anne, was interred in the Airton Meeting House burial ground in 1706.

While none of the above information gives anything more than hints and suggestions as to why a meeting house was built in Airton at the start of the seventeenth century or by whom it was used in the half-century before the local inception of Quakerism, it does portray a social and religious climate that motivated the construction in a remote Craven village of what may be the oldest dissenters' meeting place in England. It also demonstrates that when George Fox and Richard Farnsworth arrived in Craven in 1652, their preaching fitted into what were by then well-established local traditions of religious debate within which very many individuals already held religious convictions that accorded with those expounded by Fox and his associates.

3.   Midsummer 1652

A traditional, romantic view of Quaker origins is given by Elfrida Vipont Foulds (1987, pp. 13, 15). *The historic events of 1652 began when George Fox felt moved by God to climb Pendle Hill. There he saw a vision of a great people to be gathered, a vision which proved to be prophetic, for when he followed in the direction indicated, he found the Westmorland Seekers..., who were eagerly awaiting fresh light in their search for Truth.... Travelling through the Dales, George Fox came to Brigflatts, where he.... These momentous weeks saw the birth of the Society of Friends as an organized body.* Two questions require answers: Why did George Fox venture to such an out of the way place as Pendle Hill, and where did he go from there? Pendle Hill is unlikely to have been a premeditated destination. All the evidence in Fox's own writings is that he cared intensely about people and little if at all about natural scenery. Perhaps Fox and his companion, Farnsworth, had set out to visit John Webster and the people of Grindleton, or perhaps they were heading for Downham, South of Sawley in Lancashire, to meet Ralph Asheton (or Assheton), who was a member of the Long Parliament and one of Cromwell's chief men of arms. The Asheton home was held in joint tenancy with the Lister family; in 1648, Oliver Cromwell and John Lambert conferred there while the New Model Army was quartered in Downham on its way to the battle of Preston. By focussing our attention on the early stages of Fox's journey to Sedbergh in June 1652, we may obtain a more convincing, if less rose-tinted, understanding of the foundations of this religious movement.

George Fox was born in 1624 in Drayton-in-the-Clay, Leicestershire. In 1643 he completed his apprenticeship to a shoemaker who was also a sheep grazier, and left home to travel in search of religious enlightenment. Visiting the Home Counties, London, Manchester, Nottinghamshire, Derbyshire and Warwickshire, Fox entered into debates and discussions in which he gradually assumed a position of leadership among like-minded friends. (Before Quakerism became an organised movement, the appellation was generally used with a lowercase f.) The first gatherings of these friends, who were not yet called Quakers, were held in Nottinghamshire in 1647 and 1648. Fox preached about the possibility of direct communion with God and the need for sincerity and personal integrity. He opposed the ideas of predestination and universal sinfulness, and the institution of paid clergy. By 1650, when he was imprisoned in Nottinghamshire for disturbing the peace and, later the same year, in Derby for the same reason, he seems to have had a well formulated intention to start a religious movement or revival, perhaps feeling himself called to act in the manner of an Old Testament prophet. The name Quaker was first ascribed to Friends when, during his trial in Derby, Fox told Justice Bennet to *tremble at the word of God.* Probably his time in prison was used to make contacts and to plan a campaign of travels; however, we should not necessarily expect this to be recorded in any of the versions of Fox's very retrospective journals.

On his release from prison in 1651, George Fox travelled through Derbyshire, Nottinghamshire, and the East Riding of Yorkshire, visiting among many other places Balby, Cleveland, Doncaster, Hull, Pickering and York, preaching, making contacts, and finding auditors almost wherever he went. Some accepted his understanding, that God teaches his people Himself, without the need for intermediary priests, rituals, or consecrated *steeple houses* and a few of what were to become known as Quaker meetings were established. While in East Yorkshire in 1651, Fox met James Nayler, who joined with him as an itinerant Quaker preacher. Nayler was born in West Ardsley in 1618 and moved to Wakefield in 1639.

In 1643, he served as a corporal in the New Model Army under Thomas Fairfax, and in 1650 as a quartermaster under the future Major General, John Lambert. Nayler could not have accompanied Fox's travels in the West Riding in 1652 as he was by then imprisoned in Appleby. However, in discussing who would be open to this new understanding, Nayler and others with local knowledge would have spoken of the several independent religious groups and congregations in the Craven area and adjacent parts of what is now Lancashire. Foremost among those to be visited are likely to have been members of the Grindleton congregation, whichever members of the Fairfax-Lister-Tempest alliance could be persuaded to listen to them, Major General Lambert if he was at home in Calton, and Seekers including especially the Taylor brothers. Fox's arrival in time to meet the Seekers and their leaders, not at the Taylors' home in Carleton but at the midsummer hiring fair in Sedbergh would have been the result of prior knowledge and a planned schedule rather than happenstance. Fox and his friends would also have been well aware of John Lambert's and his wife's support of religious toleration.

While there are no records of the actual itinerary followed by Fox and Farnsworth and of the places where they stopped to preach, there are seventeenth- and eighteenth-century maps and records of all the major roads and pack-horse trails in our area. If we make the obvious assumption, that the two men would not usually have walked along obscure by-ways over uninhabited hills and moors, but would have followed the most frequented routes leading to the towns and villages where they were most likely to find sympathetic auditors, a most probable outline of their travels can be reconstructed. On their walk westward from an unspecified place near Bradford to Pendle Hill, Fox and his travelling companion, Richard Farnsworth (*circa* 1630 - 1666), would necessarily have passed through Skipton, where they may have spent some days. As mentioned in the previous chapter, it is likely to have been at this time that Fox met James Tennant of Scarhouse in Langstrothdale, who owned property in Skipton. These Tennants were active supporters of the Seeker community or fellowship; they soon became staunch Quakers as well as personal friends of George Fox. Most probably, it was while Fox and Farnsworth were in Skipton before continuing on to the Clitheroe area that arrangements were made for Fox to meet with leaders of the Seeker community at their annual gathering, which was to coincide with a midsummer hiring fair in Sedbergh, and an invitation extended to him to attend a private meeting of Seeker leaders at the home of Gervase Benson in Sedbergh that was to precede the larger Seeker gathering.

We have two main sources for reconstruction of the route followed by Fox and Farnsworth on their way towards Sedbergh in 1652 and for events along the way. Fox's *Journals* and William Sewel's *History of the Rise, Increase and Progress of the Christian People Called Quakers* present somewhat complementary difficulties as source material. Fox's *Journals*, several versions of which have been published, were not contemporaneous records intended to provide a neutral history. Rather, they are recollections of past events filtered through the multiple lenses of subsequent experience, self-justification, editorial prudence and the desire to create a founding narrative for a religious movement. Some, perhaps many, incidents and contacts with individuals which might have found place in a daily log were forgotten or deliberately omitted from these accounts, while others assumed in retrospect an importance which may not have been apparent when they occurred. Sewel's *History* is also indirect; he was not present at the events he records, but obtained his accounts at second hand from those who had been involved in the beginnings of Quakerism. He does, however, attempt to be comprehensive and to give a measured account of those beginnings. Sewel's *History* was compiled partly independently of Fox's *Journals*. Internal evidence implies that Richard Farnsworth was Sewel's informant for the travels from *near Bradford* at least up to the occasion when Fox and Farnsworth slept outdoors one night, perhaps somewhere between Pendle Hill and Airton: *About this time Richard Farnsworth went into an eminent steeple-house, in or about Wakefield; where he spoke so powerfully that the people were amazed.... It was well known, that G. Fox had no horse at that time, but travelled on foot. He coming now into a steeple-house not far from Bradford.... He passed from thence without much opposition, and travelled now for some time with Richard Farnsworth: with whom he once passed a night in the open field, on a bed they made of fern..... Then parting from him, he came into Wensleydale.... Thus he went from place to place, and often met with strange occurrences, some of which were more jocose than serious; others very rude, and even dangerous to his life. But he trusted in God, really believing that He had sent him to preach repentance, and to exhort people to a true conversion.... Thus travelling on, he came near Sedbergh; there he went to a meeting at Justice Benson's, where a people met that were separated from the publick worship.... most of the hearers were convinced of the Truth declared by him.... About this time there being a fair at Sedbergh, G. Fox declared the day of the Lord through the fair; and afterwards went into the steeple-house yard...* (Sewel, 1811 vol.1, pp. 87-88).

Sewel does not mention the climb up Pendle Hill, the significance of which may have been more apparent in Fox's *post facto* interpretation of the event than it was when it occurred. Perhaps the Grindletonians, some of whom lived not far from Pendle Hill, refused to listen to Fox's preaching or they listened but rejected his urging that they leave the Established Church and join with him in founding a new religious movement. Perhaps, to get over his disappointment and to shake their dust from his feet, he went for a walk and saw the hill large on the horizon. While the climb up Pendle Hill may not have been a noteworthy adventure for an energetic twenty-eight-year-old, and therefore not come to Sewel's attention, its significance could have been recognised retrospectively when Fox came to relate and record the experiences of his earlier years. Since at least the time of Moses, climbing mountains, alone, to receive inspiration from God has been something prophets did. Seeking clarity about what to do next or confirmation of his intended journey, Fox may have felt called to leave his companion at the bottom and do likewise. If he had been disappointed in his hopes of raising followers from among the Grindletonians, Fox would not have mentioned this in his later writings, which are biased towards creating and strengthening a religious movement, not with recording an autobiography in a modern sense of the word. Neither would he have felt it necessary to record that he had prior knowledge of the annual meeting of Seekers that was to take place at the Sedbergh summer fair. His reputed vision of a people waiting to be gathered – which he says occurred not on the hill, but later that evening in the inn where he was staying – may have been an envisaging or comprehending of the potential significance of an already prearranged meeting with Seeker leaders. If this premise is accepted, we can conclude that George Fox did not travel from Bradford to an inn somewhere in the approximate vicinity of Colne for the purpose of climbing Pendle Hill and we are led to ask, why did he go there? For that matter, why start at Bradford, what was his business in Yorkshire, and where did he go?

We can start to answer these questions by marshalling a few facts. In the first half of the seventeenth century, the Craven area was home to many people and congregations with independent, radical, democratic, and by contemporary standards eccentric opinions and theologies. Among the more prominent of these were the Grindletonians, based in the town of Grindleton near Colne, and the Seekers, two of whose leaders farmed land in Carleton, very near Skipton. There were also leading families, including those of Fairfax, Lister, Tempest and Lambert which supported to a greater or lesser extent local interests and sometimes relatively democratic values including religious toleration. Another significant fact is Fox's close association with James Nayler, who was a very thoughtful, intelligent and well-informed Yorkshireman. Nayler would have known of the ferment of religious and political opinions in his county, of the leading individuals who espoused them, and of the magistrates who were most inclined to give a sympathetic hearing to liberal idealists. He would particularly have known of the tolerant attitude of Major General Lambert, under whom he had served in Scotland. Farnsworth, who was from Balby near Doncaster, is also likely to have known by repute, or perhaps personally, many of the Yorkshire people who were most open to religious concepts which accorded with those which he and Fox were advocating. He may have travelled with Fox in order to facilitate introductions to some of the West Riding people and families who were most likely to give them a sympathetic hearing, but not to have continued northwards, where he perhaps lacked personal connections. If we accept that a major aim of Fox's travels in the late spring and early summer of 1652 was to speak, debate and win converts wherever they went, it becomes possible to construct his probable itinerary.

Late May or early June 1652 found Fox and Farnsworth somewhere near Bradford embarking on their travels. Unfortunately for our purposes, Fox's accounts of his itinerary omit Craven place names and seem to conflate several visits he made to Yorkshire, while Sewel's *History* mentions nothing between Bradford and Sedbergh except that Fox travelled part of the way with Farnsworth and that one night they slept in an open field, as if this were a particularly unusual circumstance; Fox also mentions this detail. As there are no more precise records of these travels and the only probable intermediate point mentioned between Pendle Hill and Brigflatts, near Sedbergh, is Scarhouse in Langstrothdale close to its junction with Upper Wharfedale, reconstructing a plausible route is the best we can do. The two men may have started near Bradford in the hope of meeting Lord Fairfax, who had been a leading figure in defending local interests, independent thought and religious toleration. The Fairfax estate at Denton was just a few miles from Ilkley. Although upon his military retirement in 1650 Fairfax had moved to his larger estate at Nunappleton, south of York, Fox and Farnsworth may have expected to find him at Denton, which Fairfax retained and probably continued to visit. Alternatively, they may have hoped for a receptive hearing from some of Fairfax's retainers or tenants who remained at Denton. Whether starting from Denton or directly from Bradford, the only practicable direct route westward was by way of Skipton, an important market town where they found attentive auditors. It would probably have been in Skipton or in nearby Carleton that Fox and Farnsworth met Seeker leaders and learned that they would be holding their annual gathering in Sedbergh to coincide with a midsummer fair, which could have provided cover for what might otherwise have been a suspect gathering. Fox's timely arrival in Sedbergh and his being invited or permitted to speak to a private gathering of Seeker leaders at the home of Gervase Benson imply that he had prior knowledge of this gathering and had scheduled his travels accordingly. Conversely, the Seekers' foreknowledge that Fox had been invited to address their annual gathering could explain how a notably large congregation including Margaret Fell, who without such an incentive would have been unlikely to attend a rustic event remote from her home near Ulverston, came to be assembled at what would otherwise have been a routine country fair. James Tennant, a Seeker who lived in Scarhouse at the top of Wharfedale and who also owned land in Skipton, is likely to have to have been among Fox's first auditors in Skipton and may have been his host a few weeks later in the late spring of 1652.

After visiting Skipton, the town of Grindleton, near Pendle Hill, would have been a most likely destination, perhaps with a stop on the way at Broughton Hall, home of the Tempest family, who in that generation were active supporters of the Parliamentary cause. From Grindleton, an almost direct and not difficult route into the Dales from the south-west was more frequently travelled in the seventeenth century than it is now. This goes by way of Gisburn and Hellifield to Otterburn, Airton and Calton, then over Calton Moor and Weets

Top to Bordley, where it joins Mastiles Lane. It enters Upper Wharfedale at Kilnsey, to the north of Threshfield and Grassington. Place names indicated on John Speed's 1610 map of Yorkshire, which may have been consulted by Fox and Farnsworth, include in an almost direct south-west to north-east line: Cledero [Clitheroe], Gisborne [Gisburn], Hellifield, Caulten [Calton] and Kilnsey, and thence in an almost straight north-westerly direction up the river Wharfe and through Langstrothdale to Dent and on to Sedbergh. A pack-horse route from Newcastle to Lancaster ran through Langstrothdale (Hartley and Ingilby, 1956, p. 42). Depending on the exact route taken, the distance from Pendle Hill to Airton and Calton is approximately fifteen miles. If Fox and Farnsworth parted company in Airton, Farnsworth may have returned to Skipton by way of Rylstone. As well as regular Quaker meetings held at Airton, probably starting in 1653, they were also held at Scale House, home of the brothers William, Edward and George Watkinson. A Quaker burial ground at Rylstone may have been in use from 1657. However, in Quaker records after 1660, Rylstone seems to have been used as a euphemistic designation to avoid mentioning Airton, and by implication any association with Major General Lambert. While it is not impossibles that Quaker meetings and interments were held both in Airton and at Rylstone in the 1650s, this is a question that invites further research. In either case, these dates imply that George Fox and Richard Farnsworth met some members of the Watkinson family in 1652, probably in the market town of Skipton before they went to Pendle Hill, perhaps also in Airton and at their home in Rylstone.

When speaking with George Fox before he set off for the Craven area, James Nayler is likely to have emphasized that Fox should visit Lambert. If the Major General's interest could be gained, Quakerism would have the support of the second most influential person in the land after Oliver Cromwell. Some years later, the Major General's wife, Frances, was reputed to have been sympathetic to Quakerism. Such an interest was more likely to have been motivated by personal contact with Quakers, including perhaps Fox, than by a perusal of contentious literature. Knowledge of and interest in Quakerism continued into the next generation of the Lambert family. Writing in 1676, the preacher John Jolly (1629-1702), who served as priest of an Independent chapel in Wymondhouses, said, *A special providence in my calling at Calton as I went to Kendale, Msts. Lambert being almost carryed away by the Quakers, the Lord was pleased to bless my endeavours for the turning of the scales, and for the fixing of her weak and wavering spirit.* The Mistress Lambert referred to in this episode was Barbara, daughter-in-law of the Major General. Her knowledge of and inclination towards Friends' principles most probably resulted from listening to Quaker preachers and to direct contact with individual Friends. Perhaps she was influenced by John Hall's persuasiveness or perhaps she sometimes attended Friends meetings in Airton, where she could have heard a variety of Quaker preachers. This incident demonstrates that members of the Lambert family must have been well aware of how the Meeting House on their land was being used and were not unsympathetic to Friends' teachings. It was Barbara Lambert's husband, the fourth John Lambert, who sold Airton Meeting House and its associated buildings to William and Alice Ellis in 1700.

There are good reasons to conclude that the Major General and his wife were residing in Calton in early June 1652, which is the very time when George Fox would have been in this area. Owing to the greatness of John Lambert, who was then at the height of his power and influence, and his well-known support for democratic causes and for religious toleration, it is more probable that Fox and Farnsworth would have gone to Calton for the purpose of meeting him and his associates than that they would have by-passed Malhamdale. The unusual presence of a purpose-built, relatively long-established Dissenters Meeting House in Airton would have been another attraction for them, and Airton or Calton might have been good places to look for refreshment or to spend the night. We may embroider this story a little by suggesting that perhaps it was late in the day when Fox and Farnsworth set out from somewhere in the neighbourhood of Pendle Hill and that the place they slept outdoors in a field was between there and Calton, it being relatively benign, cultivated country where shelter under a hedge might easily be found. If so, when they arrived in Calton, the two itinerants may have been somewhat dishevelled, which could have been unattractive to the fastidious and well-dressed Lamberts. The historian Whitaker, who was no admirer of Lambert, describes him as having been *well born, well bred, little tinctured with fanaticism, of a competent fortune, an excellent understanding, and even an elegant taste* (1878, p. 258). Rather than being offered hospitality in the manor house, Fox and Farnsworth may have preached and lodged overnight in the Airton Meeting House.

From Airton or Calton, it is an easy walk to Bordley, then along Mastiles Lane to Kilnsey and up Wharfedale. The presence of mid-seventeenth-century Quaker families at Bordley, where the Wilkinsons owned Knowlebank Farm, suggests that this was the route taken. Most probably, Fox's proximal destination was Scarhouse, near Hubberholme, the home of James Tennant, whom he may have met in Skipton a few days or weeks previously. In his memoirs, George Fox says, *So I came through the dales to a man's house, one Tennant, and I was moved to speak to the family.... and declare God's everlasting Truth to him and he was convinced, and his family, and he lived and died in the Truth.* A record made by Settle Monthly Meeting in 1704 relates that, *George Fox, at his first coming into the North, which was in the year 1652, was directed to the house of James Tennant, called Scarhouse, in Langstrothdale... where a meeting was settled and continues to this day.* The Tennants were an influential and well-connected family of yeoman farmers. Richard and Henry Tenant of Waterhouses on Malham Moor were mentioned in the previous chapter; in 1632, a Richard Tennant became vicar of Kettlewell, in Upper Wharfedale. After suffering repeated fines, distraints and imprisonments for his upholding Quaker testimonies including refusing to pay church tithes and taxes to support the militia, and refusing to swear oaths, James Tennant died in York Castle prison in 1674. The refusal to support a paid clergy and tithe farmers was a matter of principle for early Friends. The Tennants' substantial house and land were leased from the Earl of Cumberland in 1650. It included a walled plot that was first set aside for Seeker interments, but was subsequently used as a Quaker burial ground. In the next generation, the Tennants continued to be leading Quakers and their home was for many years a Friends meeting place. In 1677 it was the scene of a large gathering addressed by George Fox. There is no record of Richard Farnsworth having accompanied George Fox to Sedbergh in 1652. A likely place for them to have parted company may have been at Airton or Calton, with Farnsworth walking five miles to Rylstone, perhaps visiting William Watkinson and his brothers at Scale House before returning to Skipton and onwards from there. Walking along a well-established pack horse route up the River Wharfe, Fox would have reached Scarhouse, where he may have been entertained for some days before embarking on the more strenuous part of the route, from Langstrothdale into Dentdale. and on to Brigflatts near Sedbergh, where he met with and convinced many Seekers, including their leaders Thomas and Christopher Taylor, Gervase Benson, Margaret Fell, and others of the truthfulness of his religious insights.

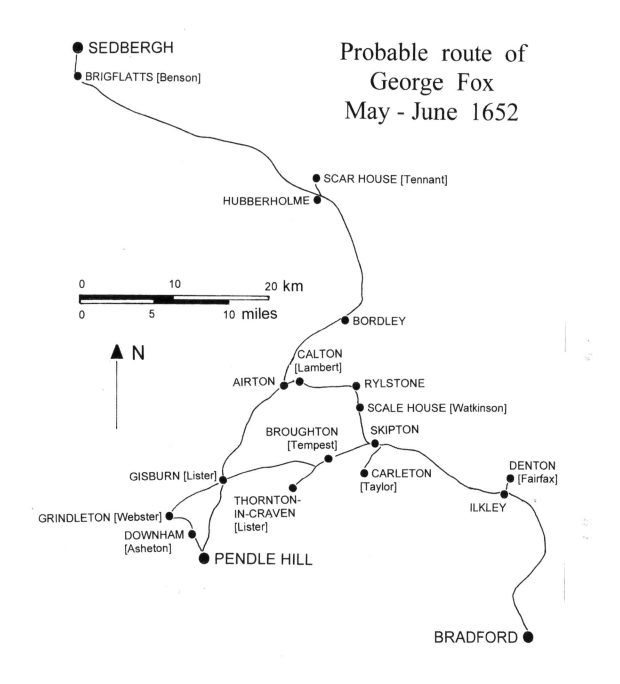

Probable route of
George Fox
May - June 1652

map by D.W. Phillipson

4.   Airton Friends in the Seventeenth Century

Architectural and other lines of evidence detailed in *Hidden in Plain Sight, History and Architecture of the Airton Meeting House* (Phillipson and Armstrong 2017) show that the Airton Meeting House was purpose-built as a semi-clandestine meeting place, possibly at the end of the sixteenth, or more probably in the first decade of the seventeenth century. Thus, it was well established when the first Quakers to visit our area, George Fox and Richard Farnsworth, came this way in 1652 on their travels northwards from Pendle Hill. Most probably, they visited Major General John Lambert at his home in the neighbouring village of Calton and preached in the Airton Meeting House. Starting soon after this visit, it was used for Quaker meetings for worship that were attended by Friends from Airton, Bordley, Cracoe, Eshton, Flasby, Hetton, and Rylstone. Its meetings were supported by visiting Quaker preachers, sometimes referred to as *First Publishers of Truth*, among whom were William Dewsbury, Richard Farnsworth, Thomas Stubbs, Miles Halhead, James Nayler and Gervase Benson. Miles Halhead was roughly treated when he preached in the marketplace in Skipton in 1654. Yearly, General and Monthly Meetings of Friends in the North were held alternately in Skipton and at Scale House and probably, as considered in this chapter, in Airton. A major regional gathering at Scarhouse in Langsthrothdale in 1677 was addressed by George Fox.

One of the first local Quaker families was that of the Watkinsons of Scale House, who were active in their support of Friends starting in 1652 or 1653. This was a family of three brothers: William, Edward, and George. William lived in the family home in Rylstone, which was then considerably smaller than it is now. Edward farmed land in Bradley, where he started a Quaker meeting, at which some years later William Ellis was *convinced* to join Friends. George Watkinson farmed land at Scotton, near Knaresborough, where he, too, founded a Quaker meeting. Other prominent Friends whose names are associated with Scale House/Rylstone/Airton Meeting are John Hall and Richard Scosthrop [or Scosterop]. Richard Scosthrop (born in 1628) is in some records credited with starting Rylstone Meeting in 1653. It is also said that at first he was a persecutor of Friends, but soon changed and became a travelling Quaker minister who preached in Scotland and elsewhere in Britain. If both of these statements, which I have not looked into, are correct, they suggest that Scosthrop had encountered and was in some sense involved with Quakerism for several years before George Fox visited Malhamdale in the summer of 1652. His family name implies a close attachment to Malhamdale, Scosthrop being the third member of the Airton-Calton-Scosthrop trinity of small villages at the lower end of Malhamdale. If Richard Scosthrop knew about Quakerism before 1652, so too might his family, his neighbours and probably many others in Malhamdale and in the wider Skipton area. This is not a surprising conclusion in view of the ease and rapidity with which people and ideas travelled throughout England during and after the Civil War period. In 1661 Richard Scosthrop, Henry Fell, and Jonathan Stubbs set out to travel to China and to visit Prester John's country [modern Ethiopia], but were unable to find shipping to carry them. Instead, Scosthrop took passage on a ship to Smyrna, but he died on board. Thomas Taylor of Carleton, the former Seeker leader, is credited with convincing the first Quaker in Countersett, Richard Robinson, that George Fox's teaching opened the way to salvation.

During the middle decades of the seventeenth century, Quaker meetings were somewhat fluid in their arrangements and designations, with Friends worshipping wherever it was convenient, often in a room in a private home, as they sometimes did at Scale House. No contemporary records of Rylstone Meetings have been found which date to the 1650s and few records mention Airton Meeting's existence in the mid-seventeenth century. In what seems to have been a defensive reaction to the Restoration of the Monarchy in 1660, mention of Airton Meeting and of the defeated and imprisoned Major General Lambert were avoided in most Quaker records and in published memoirs such as that of David Hall concerning his father's convincement. Presumably this was in support of Friends' efforts to distance themselves from their previous involvement with the New Model Army and to present themselves as peaceful, loyal subjects of the restored Monarchy. Much as Friends may have wished to disassociate themselves from whatever political implications might arise from calling attention to their association with the Lambert family, members of the Lambert family may equally have wished to avoid calling attention to their ownership of a Dissenters' meeting house. Although used since the first decade of the seventeenth century, first by Dissenters and then for Quaker worship, the Airton Meeting House, continued to be owned by Major General Lambert and his family for almost a hundred years, until it was purchased from them in 1700. There is no way the Lamberts could have failed to know how and by whom the meeting house that stood on their land, close to their dower house in Airton and only about a mile from their family home in Calton, was used. Especially before 1689, its use for legally-prohibited religious worship, sometimes for large gatherings, could not have occurred without the protection of the Major General and his family. That Airton Friends meetings were undisturbed by crowds of informers and rabble-rousers come to turf out the Quakers and destroy their property, as happened in many other early Quaker meetings (Phillipson 1988), is attested by the substantially unaltered state of the building.

In most seventeenth- and early-eighteenth- century records, Friends meetings and activity in the Airton Meeting House are anachronistically attributed to Rylstone Meeting, or to Scale House, sometimes to Knowlebank, and once to Flasby. This conflation of names and places makes it difficult to disentangle the early records of these meetings. However, we do know that until the final decades of the seventeenth century Airton Meeting House was locally unique in being an indoor space where more people could assemble to worship or to hear a visiting Quaker preacher than could be accommodated in a private house. Of the three nearest adjacent Quaker meeting houses, Rylstone Meeting House, on Raikes Road between Hetton and Rylstone, was not built until 1711. Settle Meeting House was built in 1678 and Skipton Meeting House in 1693. The stone bench that is integral to the retaining wall in front of Airton Meeting House and is contemporary with its construction implies that larger assemblies than could be accommodated inside sometimes gathered here. In 1654, George Watkinson was fined and later imprisoned for riding his horse to a Quaker meeting on a Sunday. Since he would not have gone on horseback to attend a meeting in his own home, it is most likely that he was fined for joining Friends at a meeting in the Airton Meeting House, at a distance from Scale House that would have been more convenient to ride than to walk. Allowing some time for the court proceedings to take place, the relevant Meeting would probably have been in 1653. Although based more on inference than on definitive evidence, his conviction is the earliest suggestive indication of use of the Airton Meeting House for Quaker worship that I have been able to discover. As considered above, George Fox probably preached in Airton in June 1652, while making his way northward from Pendle Hill, and reports of Rylstone Meeting having been established in 1653 most likely refer to Quaker meetings that were in fact held in the Airton Meeting House. The earliest definitive evidence that Quaker meetings were held regularly in Airton in 1657 or 1658 is in David Hall's notes on the life of his father, John Hall (1637-1719), which is considered below, in chapter six.

Additional evidence that Quaker meetings for worship were held in Airton starting in 1652 or 1653 is in a retrospective historical minute from Settle Area Meeting. In an appendix to *The Life and Correspondence of William and Alice Ellis of Airton* that was compiled by James Backhouse in 1849 (pp. 275-281), there is a transcript of a Settle Monthly Meeting minute dated the 22nd of the 10th month 1704, recording events in the origins of Quaker meetings in the area of Settle Monthly Meeting. *Before the testimony of Truth, or the way of worshipping God in spirit was published or declared ... there was much talk and discussion, of a people who were scattered up and down the country* [Yorkshire] *and more especially in the west and northern parts thereof, who differed from other people in their belief concerning the principles of religion, and worshipping of God; and in most parts they were slandered, vilified and evil spoken of.... But there were some who pondered these sayings, and were desirous to know the certainty thereof.* This may be a reference to Seekers, the somewhat ill-defined religious movement that was partly ancestral to Quakerism, and which seems to have had a major centre and its national leadership in the Skipton Area in the first half of the seventeenth century. Airton Meeting House, which predates local Quakerism by almost half a century, may have originated as a Seeker meeting place. The same minute goes on to say that: *About the year 1652-3, came several of the servants and ministers of Jesus Christ, viz. William Dewsbury, Richard Farnsworth, Thomas Stubbs, Miles Halhead, and James Nayler, and preached the everlasting Gospel, by which many were turned from darkness to light, and from the power of Satan to the power of God. And by their ministry, a meeting was gathered and settled at Scale House, near Skipton in Craven, in Yorkshire; and Truth gained ground greatly.... And the said meeting, which was gathered and settled by these faithful labourers aforementioned, now known by the name of Knowle* [Knowlebank] *Meeting, doth remain.... Likewise near about the same time, the said William Dewsbury and James Nayler, had some meetings some miles distant from Scale House aforesaid....* Knowlebank was then a small rural farmhouse near Bordley, about three miles from Airton. The Wilkinsons of Knowlebank were active Quakers who would have held frequent meetings for worship involving their family members and visitors, but there is no record of any larger or more public gatherings being held there. Knowlebank was one of many private residences that were licensed for Quaker worship when it became possible to do so in 1689. The list of Quaker meeting places licensed in 1689 also includes a *purpose built meeting house in Flasby*, for which there is no other evidence. What are we to make of these listings of a non-existent Quaker meeting house in Flasby and a non-existent meeting in Knowlebank? Most probably they and Scale House are covert references to Quaker meetings that were in fact held in the Airton Meeting House, which is approximately equidistant between the three places. Although it was not included in the 1689 list, in 1665 Airton Meeting was recorded as a constituent of Skipton Monthly Meeting.

In1677, the designations of Quaker meetings had changed: Rylstone Meeting was then recorded as encompassing particular [now called local] meetings in Airton, Cracoe, Eshton, Flasby, Hetton and Rylstone. Friends living in these villages and hamlets may have worshipped in their homes during the week, but in the Airton Meeting House on Sundays and whenever a visiting Quaker came to speak. They could not have assembled in Rylstone since Scale House, where Friends had formerly met, went out of Quaker ownership in 1677 and Rylstone Meeting House was not built until 1711. Although no mention was made in the Settle minute of 1704 quoted above of Airton Meeting or Meeting House, it continued to be used regularly for Quaker worship. Increased attendance at Quaker meetings in Airton is likely to have been the prompt that caused William and Alice Elis to refurbish the Meeting House in about 1693 and to enlarge it in 1710. A long lease on the Meeting House and burial ground were purchased from the Lambert estate by the Ellises in 1700, just a few years previous to the date of the minute quoted here, and endowed to Friends in 1706. There was no Rylstone Meeting House in the seventeenth century. The failure of this minute to say anything about how and when Quakerism began in Airton appears to have been part of a deliberate attempt to distance Friends from any association with Major General Lambert, rather than an accidental oversight. Airton's was the only Quaker meeting in our area to have a purpose-built meeting house during most of the seventeenth century. Other local meetings of which we know, including Bradley, Broughton, Carleton, Cononley, Flasby, Kildwick, Lothersdale, Scarhouse, Silsden, and Skipton usually met in private houses, perhaps sometimes in barns. Only with the passage of the Act of Toleration in 1689 were religious dissenters including Friends permitted to hold religious meetings and to own the premises in which to do so provided that they were registered and licenced. Intriguingly, Settle Monthly Meeting's record of licenced places of worship lists a number of private house, including William Ellis' house in Airton, but does not include the Airton Meeting House. Perhaps, this was because places of worship were licensed by their owners and no member of the Lambert family either wished or felt able to do so for the Quaker meeting house that was on their land. At first, there were many Quaker meetings in the north of England, but few elsewhere. Between 1657 and 1660, regional and national gatherings of Quaker leaders were held in or near Skipton, including at Scale House (or Airton?). These meetings, which are discussed in chapter seven, were precursors of the Quaker Yearly Meetings that came to be held in London. Beginning in that decade, the Quaker movement gradually assumed a more settled and organised character with small local, or particular, meetings grouped into regional or monthly meetings. The spread of Quakerism in Yorkshire was fostered by enthusiastic, sometimes eloquent, and sometimes turbulent preaching supplemented by the active dissemination of printed materials. By 1673, Yorkshire Friends had an agreement with the York bookseller, Thomas Waite, to manage the acquisition and distribution of Quaker books.

Between 1654 and 1706, hundreds of Quakers in Yorkshire were fined, imprisoned, and had their goods and livestock distrained on account of their refusals to conform to the requirements of the Established Church, pay church tithes, or swear oaths of loyalty, and for their persistence in attending unlicensed Quaker meetings for worship. In the eleventh and twelfth months of 1660/61, as many as 229 Friends in the West Riding and 126 in the North Riding were imprisoned for refusing to take an oath of loyalty; in all, 535 Friends were imprisoned in York Castle and elsewhere that year. Ten years later, in 1670, fines totalling £2,266 14s 4d were distrained from Friends in Yorkshire. In 1683, fifty Quakers were arrested in Leeds. In 1685, a petition for relief was sent to the King by 279 Quakers imprisoned in York Castle. During this time, imprisonments and heavy distraints affected Friends in Bentham, Clapham, Farfield, Farnley, Gargrave, Giggleswick, Keighley, Low Bentham, Otley, Settle, Silsden, Skipton, Steeton, and Westhouse. While Besse's (1753) compilation of the most notable persecutions and tribulations suffered by Friends before the 1689 Act of Toleration includes multiple instances from Skipton, Gargrave, Settle, Giggleswick and one from Flasby, it includes none from Airton, nor from Rylstone or Hetton. According to local records, the Quakers John Hall of Airton and William Anderson of Kirkby Malham had property taken by bailiffs in 1678 on account of their refusals to pay church tithes. Other Malhamdale Friends who suffered fines and impositions for their Quaker testimonies included John Squire of Airton, who had 20 stooks of barley taken, and Thomas Hall of Airton, who had wool and lambs taken, both in 1682, for refusing to pay church tithes. Simeon Wilkinson of Knowlebank Farm also suffered repeatedly for his Quaker testimonies. Since these distraints are not recorded by Besse, the value of goods taken may not have been grossly disproportionate to the amount that was claimed for such dues. Another of the relatively few instances of distraints recorded within the Lambert area of land ownership and influence is that in 1683 *William Anderson, of Malon, in the parish of Kirkly Mallondale* [Kirkby Malham] was indicted at the Skipton Sessions for refusing to attend public worship. He had a mare, hay, a cart, malt and household goods worth £20 seized to pay a fine of £5 12s. That Malhamdale Friends were less affected by religious persecution than were Quakers in many other areas may have been due to the benign influence of John Lambert and his family. Until his own imprisonment in 1660, Quaker meetings in Airton seem to have been shielded by Major General Lambert. Subsequently, as royalist and establishment interests became increasingly powerful, Friends in Malhamdale were sometimes penalised for such offences as not paying church tithes, failing to attend the Established Church services, holding their own (unlicensed) religious meetings, and for refusing to swear in court or take a loyalty oath.

A letter written by William Ellis to *Simeon Wilkinson with the rest of my servants* on the *16th of the fifth month* 1697 makes it clear that meetings for worship were then held twice weekly in the Airton Meeting House: *it should be often in your thoughts, the care that hath been upon my mind for keeping week-day meetings* (Backhouse, 1849 pp. 29-30). He was most concerned that his young apprentices should not be permitted to sleep during what may have been long, silent meetings. Simeon Wilkinson, to whom this letter was addressed, was probably a son of the Quaker Richard Wilkinson of Knowlebank, Bordley, a few miles from Airton. A Simeon Wilkinson signed an epistle sent from a General Meeting of Quaker leaders on the 29th of June 1659, and the first three recorded Quaker burials at Airton are of members of the Wilkinson family, starting with Isabell Wilkinson of Knowlebank in 1663; Sarah Wilkinson, *sister of Simeon*, was buried at Airton in 1675. While it would have been practicable for Ellis' employees to walk a few yards across the road to attend mid-week worship in the Airton Meeting House, it would have been too disruptive of the weaving business for them to have travelled further. In another letter written on the *24th of the sixth month* 1697, William Ellis says, *I gave you a hint before, how I had got up a meeting house; but now shall give a small account of the good service we have had since we got it in order. Many public-friends come to us, and great numbers of people at times....* (Backhouse, 1849 p. 33). The meaning of *got up* was that some time previously, probably in about 1693, the Meeting House was refurbished and, as he says, *got in order.* Had the Ellises in fact built the meeting house, he would have said so. In a letter dated 9th of the ninth month 1698, addressed to *the Friends appointed as Overseers of the Church at Airton*, William Ellis offers general advice: *I wish your love may increase to the poor, and fatherless, and widows.... Let Friends meet often together... and see that Satan be withstood, who leads men to sleep and to idleness.... labour for that which makes for peace.... If this come to your hand, and it be seen good, read it in your First-day meeting* (Backhouse, 1849. pp 95-98). On the same day as William Ellis, who was then visiting Friends in Boston, North America, wrote the letter just quoted, his wife, Alice, addressed a letter to him in which she describes meetings for worship in Airton: *Dear and Loving Husband.... I have received six letters from thee since thou took shipping, and they were all great gladness to my mind, and especially thy last, dated the 26th of the 5th mo. last.... And many precious seasons we enjoy in the presence of God, with the many faithful messengers whom he hath drawn in his love, to visit us... and it is a gladdening to my heart to see Truth prosper...* (Backhouse, 1859 pp. 98-100). These letters comprise some of the varied strands of evidence that demonstrate that Airton Friends Meeting House was in existence and Airton Meeting thriving well before 1700. If the Meeting House had been built only recently, it would not have required refurbishment in about 1693. During most of the second half of the seventeenth century, there would have been constant visiting and marriages between Malhamdale Friends and their contemporaries in Skipton, Upper Wharfedale and Langstrothdale, as well as favouring one another in business dealings and the placing of youths in apprenticeships. The Quakers Richard Wilkinson, son of Simeon Wilkinson of Knowlebank, and Margaret Hall, daughter of John Hall of Airton, were married under the care of Settle Monthly Meeting in 1677.

A letter written by George Fox in 1689 (Barclay pp. 311-7) is germane to understanding the early development of Quakerism in the Skipton / Malhamdale / Upper Wharfedale area, and so worth quoting here at length. This letter makes it clear that during Quakerism's first decade, there was an almost constant stream of Friends with seemingly boundless energy and enthusiasm present in our area, holding meetings for worship, preaching and debating with all who cared to listen. *The first Monthly Meeting was on this wise in the North:- though we did meet concerning the poor, and to see that all walked according to the Truth, before we were called Quakers.... in 1653 in Cumberland many of the Elders came to me at Swarthmore in Lancashire, and desired that they might have a Monthly Meeting... and they had a meeting settled there for the same purpose.... Then after when the Truth was spread in Cheshire, Lancashire, Westmorland, Cumberland, Northumberland, Bishoprick and Yorkshire, and the edge of Wales, there was a meeting at Swarthmore, of some of the Elders of most of these places; where we did consider to have Monthly Meetings ordered by the power of the Lord, in most of these places.... And then there was a Yearly Meeting settled at Skipton in Yorkshire, for all the northern and southern counties; where in the wisdom of God, they did see that all walked according to the glorious gospel of God, and that there was nothing wanting among them; and if there was, one county assisted another, either in relieving the poor (in the Lord's counsel,) or in advice in sufferings, or in any other matters. The substantial men and Elders in the Truth came to the Yearly Meeting at Skipton, both from Bristol and London, and other places.... And from thence, it was removed to London the next year....*

The spread of Quakerism in Yorkshire was fostered by enthusiastic, sometimes eloquent, and sometimes turbulent preaching supplemented by the active dissemination of printed materials. It was only with the passing of the Act of Toleration in 1689 that religious dissenters including Friends were permitted to hold meetings and to own the premises in which to do so. Among the first places licensed for Quaker worship in our area were meeting houses, homes and barns in Addingham (Farfield), Arncliffe, Bellbusk, Barnoldswick, Bentham, Broughton, Carleton, Clapham, Cracoe, Dent, Earby, Gargrave, Hetton, Kildwick, Marton, Mitton, Rylstone, Salterforth, Sedbergh, Slaidburn, Settle, Skipton, Stainforth, and Thornton. Knowlebank, the Wilkinson farmhouse near Bordley was licensed and so, too, according to a West Riding Quarter Sessions record of 1689 was William Ellis's house in Airton. Both of these were two-storey cottages with small rooms which could not easily have accommodated more than a few visitors at a time. Airton Meeting House was not included in this list of Settle Monthly Meeting's licensed places for Quaker worship, but intriguingly a purpose-built meeting house at Flasby was listed. I have not found any further mention or record of a Quaker meeting house in Flasby. The most parsimonious explanation of these errors in listing is that the Airton Meeting House was incorrectly recorded as located in Flasby. We know both from the mute testimony of its architecture and from William Ellis's letter of 1697, quoted in this chapter and further discussed in chapter eight, that there was a well-established, purpose-built Meeting House in Airton. In that letter, he says that he had refurbished the Meeting House a few years previously, not that he built it; he also says that they sometimes had *great meetings*, which could not have been accommodated in his home. When Scale House went out of Quaker ownership in 1675, the Quaker meeting which had been held there changed its name to Rylstone Meeting, though it must in fact have met in the Airton Meeting House until 1711, when a new Quaker meeting house (now a private dwelling on Raikes Road) between Hetton and Rylstone was built alongside an older Quaker burial ground (probably in use from 1677). Increased attendance at local Quaker meetings seems to have prompted refurbishment of the Airton Meeting House in 1693 or 1694, the addition of its gallery and new stables in 1710, and the construction of Rylstone Meeting House in 1711.

5.   The Lamberts of Calton Hall

Among those who prospered from the sixteenth-century dismantling of the monastic estates was John Lambert of Calton, great-grandfather of Major General John Lambert, whom George Fox and others referred to as *one of the greatest in the land*, on account of his leading role during the Protectorate. In 1528, the first John Lambert was Steward of Henry Clifford first Earl of Cumberland. He acquired Airton Manor in 1530. Profiting from his position as Steward of the Privy Courts, he obtained the former holdings of Bolton Priory in Malham, Airton, Scosthrop, Otterburn and Hellifield. By 1543 he was appointed Secretary to the Council of the North. His son, the second John Lambert, further extended the family's Calton estate and was noted for his enthusiastic building activities. The manor of Kirkby Malham was purchased in 1597. Complicated inheritance settlements and legal disputes in the early seventeenth century led to a decline in the family fortune, exacerbated by a slump in wool prices. By 1629, the manors of Calton, Airton, Kirkby Malham, Hanlith, Malham East and Malham West, all owned by the Lambert family, were leased out mainly to members of the Lister, Heber and Tempest families. On the death of Josias Lambert, father of the future Major General, in 1632 the Lambert estate had clear title only to Calton Hall, and to lands in Airton held in a widow's jointure worth £30 a year. Airton Meeting House and its burial ground are on the small portion of the estate which remained in the family's immediate possession. It may have been Josias Lambert who constructed the Airton Meeting House sometime between 1597 and the mid 1620s. He apparently had radical and Dissenter sympathies and was reputed to be an enthusiastic builder,

The young John Lambert (1619-1684), the third of this name, probably received his early education from Nicholas Walton, priest and licensed master of Kirkby Malham School. Walton was reported in a visitation of 1632 for such radical practices as not wearing a surplice, and was ejected from his position as parish priest at the time of the Restoration. At the age of thirteen, the orphaned and semi-impoverished, but well-connected boy was placed by his father's will in the care of Sir William Lister of Thornton Hall, Thornton-in-Craven. Whitaker's description of the political sympathies of a younger member of the Lister family gives by implication a good description of those of his parents. *Martin Lister was born in or about the year 1638....The example and instruction of a court physician redeemed him from the disloyalty of his family; and he met with an early reward of fidelity... by royal mandate in the year of the Restoration....* (Whitaker, 1878 p. 124). In other words, earlier generations of the Listers, including those among whom the future Major General was raised, opposed the Royalist cause and did not support the Restoration. John Lambert and Frances Lister, daughter of Sir William Lister, were married in 1638. This marriage extended and strengthened Lambert's connections to several leading Yorkshire families who were part of a faction that opposed attempts to increase royal power in the north and who advocated religious toleration or maintained their Roman Catholic faith: Fairfax (of Denton, near Ilkley, and Fewston, west of Harrogate), Belasyse, Aske, Lister, and Tempest (of Broughton Hall, near Skipton). Later events were to show that Frances Lister was a very capable and determined person who developed friendships with people of radical and Quakerly inclination. All of these influences would have strengthened the future Major General's own advocacy of religious toleration, although they do not seem to have inclined him very strongly towards any particular religious sect or opinions (Dawson, 1938. p. 167).

In 1642, John Lambert served under Lord Fairfax in the Northern Association Army. During the Civil War he defeated Royalist forces in Gargrave and those attacking Thornton

Hall, but could not prevent them storming his own Airton Hall and taking 60 prisoners to Skipton Castle. The site formerly occupied by Airton Hall, the Lambert dower house, is marked by a raised mound in the field immediately north of Ellis House, directly across the road from the Airton Meeting House. Lambert was involved with the army revolt and the settlement offered to Charles I in 1647 and was largely instrumental in the conquest of Scotland in 1650 – 1651. He was the principal drafter of the *Instrument of Government* that was adopted in December 1653, whereby Oliver Cromwell was made Lord Protector. As he was an outspoken and determined advocate of religious toleration, the wording of clauses 35, 36 and 37 of the *Instrument*, which are very nearly the same as those of the 9th article of the *Agreement of the People* presented to the House of Commons in January 1648/9, may have been Lambert's own.... *that the Christian religion, as contained in the Scriptures, be held forth and recommended as the public profession of these nations.... that to the public profession held forth none shall be compelled by penalties or otherwise.... that such as profess faith in God by Jesus Christ (though differing in judgement from the doctrine, worship or discipline publicly held forth) shall not be restrained from, but shall be protected in, the profession of the faith and exercise of their religion....*

James Nayler, from West Ardsley near Wakefield, who was initially a close friend of George Fox and who became a leading member of the first generation of Quakers, served under Lambert as his quartermaster during the campaign into Scotland. Others of Lambert's associates who became early Friends included John Hodgson of Threshfield who was a captain and surgeon under Lambert, Mark Grime who was a close political ally of and deputy Lieutenant Colonel under Lambert, and Amor Stoddart. The famous radical, John Lilburne, who served under Lambert in the Parliamentary army, eventually joined Friends. Captain Adam Baynes, an associate of John Lambert and correspondent of Frances Lambert, was a member of Parliament and a magistrate who by 1655 was particularly friendly to Quakers. Another of Lambert's associates was the religious radical John Webster, who as curate of Kildwick-in-Craven in 1634 had been much influenced by the Grindletonian followers of Roger Brearley. Webster served as a chaplain under Lambert and was closely associated with another radical, William Erbury, who was also in Lambert's regiment in 1647. Both Webster and Erbury influenced the thought of early Quakers. A statement by Webster in his *The Saints Guide* of 1653 parallels clause 37 of the *Instrument of Government*, quoted above. David Boulton (2002, pp. 89-101) names other early Quakers who were officers of the New Model Army, most of whom would have been associates of, or at least known to, the Major General. One among them was Gervase Benson, a Seeker leader who became a very effective Quaker preacher. Both Webster and Benson influenced the people and events reconstructed here. Probably George Fox travelled to the Pendle Hill area in order to visit the congregation at Grindleton where Brearley and Webster had been preachers. In the mid to late 1650s, Benson made several visits to Rylstone and to Skipton; concerning one of these, he wrote that he preached in a barn in a field in Airton, which is what the Airton Meeting House would then have resembled.

Lambert was appointed Lord Deputy and Commander in Chief of Ireland in January 1652, and in February he was recalled from Scotland to prepare for this appointment. These preparations included his purchase in early May of a palatial house in Wimbledon, Surrey. However, according to Phillips (1938, p. 328), it was only two days later, on the nineteenth of May, that the appointment to Ireland was rescinded and given instead to Charles Fleetwood, the fiancé of Cromwell's recently-widowed daughter, Bridget Ireton. There is a report that, soon after this change of appointment, Lambert's wife, Frances, and Bridget Ireton quarrelled in public, in St James's Park in London, over who should yield precedence to whom and, by implication, which of them had the higher social standing (Dawson, 1938 p. 149). This would have been shortly before Bridget's marriage to Charles Fleetwood on the eighth of June. Resulting from these events, it seems likely that the Lamberts would then have left London while they considered what to do next and in order to avoid attending Bridget's wedding. Their newly-purchased Wimbledon House is unlikely to have been immediately ready for them to move into and it may not have been politic for them to do so right away. Most probably they returned to the family home in Calton in late May or early June. Further evidence that they were living in Calton in 1652 comes from David Farr (pers. com. 2010), *A firm date is of Lambert arriving in London from Calton on 19th November* [1652] (*Thurloe State Papers*, I, 589, 610). *He had certainly been in Yorkshire for up to 6 weeks before this....*[also] *Lambert was at his estate in late 1653.... From December 1653 he was based in London with the establishment of the Protectorate.* The Major General's whereabouts in early June 1652 are of particular interest since, in order to arrive in time for the midsummer hiring fair at Sedbergh, it must have been in late May or early June that George Fox passed this way after climbing Pendle Hill. An intention of meeting Lambert at Calton may have been a significant factor in the planning of Fox's itinerary.

With the ending of the Protectorate, Lambert's history is a sad one of lifelong imprisonment. His daughter, Frances, married John Blackwell (1624-1701), who had been a captain in the New Model Army in the 1650s. Blackwell looked after the Lambert family affairs. In the year Lambert died, 1684, Frances and her husband moved to North America. Although he was not a Friend, Blackwell was appointed by William Penn to serve as governor of the Quaker colony of Pennsylvania from 1688 to 1690. Farr (1999 p. 232 footnote 22) cites evidence of contact between the Major General's family and William Penn's father and a visit of Blackwell's wife, Frances (Lambert), to William Penn. The Major General's other daughters, Anne and Elizabeth, married Daniel Parrott and John Hooke, respectively. They were much involved with land dealings in East and West New Jersey, particularly a scheme started in 1684, of which Daniel Cox (governor of West New Jersey from 1687 to 1692) was at the centre. The Major General's son, a fourth John Lambert, retained some of the family lands in Malhamdale and continued to live in their manor house in Calton. Reports of the correspondence between him and his sisters may have enabled people living in Calton and Airton to be particularly aware of events and opportunities in the New World. It was this (the fourth) John Lambert's wife whom the dissenting priest, John Jolly, reported that he dissuaded from becoming a Quaker at some unspecified date before 1676. Airton Meeting House and burial ground together were purchased by William and Alice Ellis from this John Lambert in 1700 and endowed to Quaker trustees in 1706. He was survived only by a married daughter. As the last male member of the family, the direct line of Lambert inheritance was extinguished with his death in 1701. His impending demise and the anticipated sale of the Lambert estate in Malhamdale are likely to have been the reasons for the Ellises purchasing the property, almost half a century after Friends first began using it. It is this purchase of the Airton Meeting House, not its construction, that is commemorated by the initials and datestone over the Meeting House door.

6. John Hall of Airton

Born in Airton, John Hall (1637-1719) completed his apprenticeship as a tailor and returned to Airton in 1657. Soon thereafter he began to attended Quaker meetings, at one of which he heard Gervase Benson preach. It may have been while he was attending a General Meeting of Friends in the North in the autumn of 1657, that Gervase Benson spoke in the Airton Meeting House, where his ministry so impressed John Hall. Benson was also present at General Meetings held at Scale House and in Skipton on the 11th of March and on the 24th of June 1658; he signed an epistle sent from Scale House on the 11th of March 1658. The events which led to John Hall attending Quaker meetings in Airton and to his joining Friends are related in a short memorial by his son, David, who kept a Quaker boarding school in Skipton (Hall 1758). The account by David Hall indicates that the Quaker meeting in Airton was already well established when his father first visited it and that meetings for worship were held frequently, sometimes in silence, sometimes with the spoken ministry of a prominent Friend. These gatherings took place neither in the open air nor in a domestic room, but in a meeting house furnished with seating and with its own external door opening directly into the meeting room, as ours still does. Nothing in the account suggests that such meetings were then a novelty or that they had been recently initiated. This account is our best attested and second oldest evidence of an early Quaker meeting in Airton. *Now it so happened that a Friend, one Gervase Benson, had a Meeting near unto the Place* [Airton] *where my Father lived; he therefore being minded to go to the Meeting, went and found them sitting in Silence, which seemed to him a strange Thing, and not knowing the Advantage thereof, he retreated and walked into the Fields: A while after returning near the Meeting-place, the Friend Gervase was declaring, he therefore approach'd, and leaning his Head to the Door-post, was so reach'd that Tears trickled down his Cheeks; notwithstanding which, being some time after at a silent Meeting, he was uneasy with it, but resolv'd to go one Meeting more, and if there were no Words, he thought to go no more: So he went, and standing at the Door, Friends beckon'd him that he might come in and sit among them; he thereupon sat down with them in Silence, but presently the Power of the Lord seiz'd upon him, and broke him down, so that he was fully convinc'd of the blessed Truth in that silent Meeting, and never turn'd his Back thereon to his dying Day.* This passage refers to two or three Quaker meetings for worship held in the mid-1650s in the Airton Meeting House, which was then a barn-like single room.

Following his convincement to Quaker *Truth*, John Hall refused any longer to make decorative or luxury clothing because he found that to do so was inconsistent with Friends' simplicity of lifestyle. He undertook plain work only and most of his employers respected the stand he took.... *whereas aforetime he had gratify'd the vain Minds of Men and Women in the Fashions and Superfluities then in Vogue, now he found a Restriction laid upon him, and a conscientious Scruple in doing such like Things..... Soon after this he was sent for by a great Man, to go to his House to make up some fine Cloaths: When he and his Man came to the Place and saw the Work, behold it was very fine, and to be wrought with many Superfluities, which for Conscience sake he durst not undertake..... He freely turned his Back of all that worldly Interest, and Providence so favour'd his conscientious Care, that he got plain Work enough, and his Wages increas'd , and as he was faithful in a little, the Lord made greater Things manifest unto him....* The *great Man* referred to was Major General Lambert, whom Friends continued to avoid naming. Both Lambert and his wife, Frances, strongly supported the Parliamentary cause, but not that of the Puritan sectaries. When opportunity permitted, they dressed and lived much more like Cavaliers than like Roundheads.

During the remainder of his life, John Hall continued to be active in upholding Friends' principles and was reputed to be an eloquent and persuasive speaker. David Hall goes on to relate of his father that, *In his early Days, soon after his Convincement, a weighty Concern came upon his Mind, To go to the Steeple-house, and stand before the Priest, while he was speaking in the Pulpit, under whose Ministry aforetime he had often sat; to which Concern he gave up, and, going into the Steeple-house* [Kirkby Malham church], *stood by the Priest, and with a steady Countenance silently fix'd his Eyes upon him, wherewith the Priest was so confounded, that he called out to the Wardens to come and take him away; but they knowing him to be a sober Neighbour, and seeing him stand still and silent were not hasty to execute the Priest's Command; whereupon the Priest being wholly at a Stop and Non-plus, beginning to close his Book, cries out, If you will not come and take him away, I will take him away myself. Then the Wardens, or some of the People, put him out of Doors. The Priest fell to his Work again, and my Father came in again at a Back-door, and found it his place silently to face the Priest, as before, at which the Priest being a second time confounded, they put him again out of Doors: After a little while the Congregation were dismissed, and he cleared himself among* [preached to] *the People in the Grave-yard.... Many other Exercises he had in Great Men's Houses, through with the Lord was pleased to lead him gently and safely, ... And although he came forth, as it were in a Winter Season, when the Penal Laws were on Foot, he was not discouraged, but willingly suffered the spoiling of his Goods for Truth's sake; when he was very low in the World, the Informers took from him a Mare, on which he used to ride to Meetings. After some Time he removed to Skipton, where he bore a living Testimony to the Truth, both in Doctrine and in Conversation.* His *Exercises in Great Men's Houses* may have included discussions with or preaching to members of the Lambert household.

In about 1680, John Hall moved to Skipton, where he kept a temperance inn, had his goods and family possessions distrained for the non-payment of church tithes, and was briefly imprisoned several times for attending Quaker meetings. In November 1682, eighteen Skipton Friends were fined a total of £44 for attending an illegal religious meeting. John Hall was fined £9 for speaking at that meeting and would have been fined £20 had he been able to pay that much. He was closely involved with the building of Skipton Meeting House, which was completed in 1693. His son, David Hall, kept a Quaker boarding school in Skipton from about 1703 to 1757.

7.   The Early Organisation of Friends
(by Richard Harland and Laurel Phillipson)

Between 1656 and 1660, general and regional meetings of Quakers were held in the North. In addition to eight or nine that were held in Skipton and at Scale House (or Airton?), such meetings were held at Balby, at Scarhouse near Hubberholme, in Kendal, and at Swarthmoor Hall near Ulverston in Cumbria. Reminiscing in later life, George Fox recollected that Skipton and Scale House were the primary centres. Some of these gatherings were attended only by the most active leaders and travelling ministers of the rapidly evolving movement that became the Religious Society of Friends; they included Thomas Aldam, Gervase Benson, William Dewsbury, Richard Farnsworth, George Fox, Thomas Goodaire, Miles Halhead, Thomas Killam, Thomas Lawson, James Nayler, Thomas Stubbs, and Thomas Taylor. Other meetings were more widely attended. These various meetings may have repeated or reflected an informal but effective system of organisation pioneered by the Seekers. Several of the most energetic and influential of the early Quaker preachers, including Gervase Benson and Thomas Taylor, had originally been Seeker leaders. Starting in 1654, a Kendal Fund for "the service of Truth" helped to defray the costs of Friends who travelled to these meetings.

A very widely attended meeting was held at Skipton on Wednesday the 25th of April 1660. Dictating his Journal in 1673 – 74, George Fox recalled that towards the end of the year 1656, *I was moved of the Lord to send for one or two out of a county to* [come to] *Swarthmoor and to set up the men's* [monthly] *meetings… and to settle that meeting at Skipton concerning the affairs of the church which continued till 1660…. Friends did come out of most parts of the nation… about business… both in this nation and beyond the seas….* In 1689, again pondering old times, he dictated, *some short heads and memorandums to Friends that have not known the beginning of it…. Then there was a Yearly Meeting settled at Skipton in Yorkshire for all the northern and southern counties, where in the wisdom of God they did see that all walked according to the glorious gospel of God, and that there was nothing wanting among them, and if there was, one county assisted another…, either in relieving the poor (in the Lord's counsel) or in advice in sufferings, or any other matters ….* Some of the concerns discussed at the Skipton meeting in April 1660 were: the establishment of a regular system of monthly and general meetings, care for their own poor, watching over the integrity and conduct of members, and fundraising to assist the families of Friends imprisoned for witnessing to *the Truth,* which was the term used by Quakers to summarise their sense of religious values and integrity. They also recorded the distribution of loaves of bread to large numbers of poor people. They did not record what may have been their most pressing concern: the perilous situation of Friends as individuals and of the Quaker religious movement with respect to the turbulent national political situation, restoration of the Monarchy and the arrest of Major General Lambert. An epistle sent out from the meeting was signed by 98 Friends, including Samuel Watson of Stainforth, Thomas Taylor of Carleton, William Watkinson of Scale House and Symon Wilkinson of Knowlebank. With hindsight, this meeting can be recognised as the first Quaker Yearly Meeting. A probable outcome that may have been discussed, but which was not recorded in any minute or epistle, was that Quakers began to emphasise their peaceable inclinations and to avoid calling attention to the previous involvement of many individual Friends with the Parliamentary army and with the defeated Major General Lambert. Subsequent Quaker Yearly Meetings were held in London, starting in 1668.

In the generally accepted list of 12 women and 54 men who were most active in the early spread of Quakerism, and who are sometimes referred to as the Valiant Sixty [*sic*], all came from Yorkshire or Cumbria. In 1654, a London Friend wrote of the expectation that some of these northerners would soon come to spread the word in the south. Soon thereafter another London Friend wrote that they were being invaded by *plaine north country ploughmen.* Thirty-four of the 66 early Quaker leaders were farmers or involved in associated trades, and much of the early Quaker insistence on plain dress and plain speech was little more than the maintenance of generally prevalent country customs of northern England. Such was the local effectiveness of Quaker advocacy of a knowledge of God attained through direct personal experience rather than from external preaching and teaching, that by 1660 there were ten local meetings of Quakers in the area now encompassed by the Craven and Keighley Area Meeting. All five of our present local meetings, Airton, Bentham, Keighley, Settle and Skipton, were established by that date, but only Airton had a purpose-built meeting house, which continued to be owned by Major General Lambert and his family. However, in order to avoid calling attention to Friends' previous involvement with the New Model Army in general and with Lambert in particular, neither the Airton Meeting House nor the Major General figure in Quaker records compiled after 1660. When the system of particular (subsequently known as preparative and now known as local) meetings was first established, Scale House and Rylstone were given nominal preference over Airton.

In 1660, Skipton was a market town of about 200 households and 1,000 inhabitants where, in 1652, the Countess of Pembroke received the rent from 1 mill, 1 dye works, 17 *shoppes*, 4 *chambers,* and from 94 tenants of cottages, houses, fields and closes, some with multiple dwellings (Dawson, 1882 pp. 198-201). Local magistrates were relatively tolerant, and dissidents including Grindletonians and Seekers were numerically well represented. By the time George Fox and Richard Farnsworth visited Skipton in 1652, Fox had been travelling and preaching for about five year. Since news travelled almost as rapidly in mid-seventeenth-century England as it does today and debates about religion were a pressing concern for many people, some residents of the Skipton area are likely to have known something about Quaker thought and Quaker preaching before the first Quaker preachers arrived in 1652 and 1653. Scarhouse, Scale House, Carelton and Airton were each centres of radical thinking from well before the arrival of Fox and Farnsworth. From an early date, the Watkinson brothers made Scale House a hospitable centre for Quakers. It had easy bridleway access from several directions and a commodious meeting house a few miles away in Airton. Its reputation attracted a galaxy of men from amongst the Valiant Sixty, including William Dewsbury from Allerthorpe near Pocklington, Richard Farnsworth from Tickhill south of Doncaster, James Nayler from Ardsley also near Doncaster, Thomas Stubbs from Dalston near Cockermouth, and Miles Halhead from Underbarrow near Kendal. George Fox may have visited Scale House in 1652; he most probably did visit Calton and Airton that year. Of Friends living in Skipton town in the 1650s we know less. Quaker truth spread through a radical network of independent craftsmen like Thomas Oddy and farmers like Edward Wilberfoss. A few miles from Skipton, in Carleton, a group of Seekers was nurtured into a Quaker meeting by Thomas Taylor, and in Bradley a Quaker meeting was established and supported by members of the Watkinson family. Thomas Lawson stayed with the Wilkinson family at Knowlebank in Bordley in 1658 while he attended a general meeting at Scale House.

Preceding a Yearly Meeting of Friends in Skipton in 1660, regional gatherings of representative Friends from a wide area (General Meetings) were held at Scale House or in Skipton in 1657, 1658, 1659, and 1660. A General Meeting held at Durham on the 1st October 1659 sent an epistle to the Skipton General Meeting held on the 5th October 1659, proposing the establishment of *one General Meeting of* [all] *England....* The gatherings we know of that were held at Scale House or at Skipton are listed here. In the 1650s, Scale House was not the large house it is today. While it would have accommodated small groups, any larger gatherings associated with these meetings would most probably have been convened in in Airton, or in Skipton.

1657, *in the autumn of the year*, at Scale House. The Scale House epistle was addressed from the North to the South and looks to be smoothing out some misunderstanding, *… seeing that the former paper that went from the North was not owned by all in the South,… we* [are] *free to acquaint you with what we have done…. [We] find great service in this General Meeting, which we purpose to continue as often as we can. … We have also settled a way for collections amongst ourselves, and for ordering other outward things, that all may be preserved in peace and order.*

1658, 11 March, at Scale House. Thos Lawson was there and wrote to Margaret Fell…. *this day was a meeting at Scale House, there was several friends,* [including] *Gervase Benson, Thos Goodaire…. About the 13 of this month a meeting is appointed at Skipton.* Thomas Lawson (1630-91), Cambridge-educated and an ordained clergyman, resigned his living when convinced of the Truth and established a school at Great Strickland near Lancaster. Later he became a noted botanist. Writing from Bordley in 1658, he would have lodged probably with the Wilkinsons of Knowlebank, but possibly with the Proctors of Bordley Hall, each about 6 miles from Scale House and little more than half that distance from Airton. Gervase Benson (*ob.* 1679) had legal skills and under Charles I was a magistrate and mayor of Kendal. He was now living in Sedbergh, modestly styling himself husbandman. Maybe it was on this occasion that he addressed the meeting at Airton which began the convincement of John Hall, who went on to do great work for Friends in Malhamdale and in Skipton and who master-minded the erection of Skipton meeting house in 1693. Thomas Goodaire had been convinced by George Fox in 1651 and by 1658 had already been in prison in Worcester and in Northampton for witnessing in the Truth; he died in 1693.

1658, about 13 March, at Skipton. The evidence for this meeting is Thomas Lawson's letter quoted above. The two meetings in March, perhaps each of just a handful of Friends, doubtless prepared for the next meeting at Scale House.

1658, 24 June, at Scale House. Friends were invited from the ten northern counties of England. Their concluding epistle is an eloquent fundraising letter. *Having heard of great things done by the mighty power of God in many nations beyond the seas, whither He has called forth many of our dear brethren and sisters to preach the everlasting Gospel… who are now in strange lands in great straits and hardships in the daily hazard of their lives… we do therefore in the unity of the Spirit and bond of Truth cheerfully agree… to move and stir up the hearts of Friends… freely and liberally to offer up unto God of their earthly substance… to be speedily sent up to London… that the hands of those who are beyond the seas in the Lord's work may be strengthened….*

It was said of the 42 signatories to this letter that *no weightier list of solid Friends from the North could have been compiled.* Amongst those signing were the following. Thomas Aldam (*c.* 1616-1660) of Warmsworth, now within Doncaster, was one of the first Quakers imprisoned in York Castle, in 1651. Thomas Atkinson (*c.* 1604-1684) of Cartmel did prison terms for not paying tithes. Oliver Atherton of Ormskirk died in prison, for tithe refusal, in 1663. Thomas Brocksopp probably came from Derbyshire. Thomas Killam (*ob.* 1690) and his brother John Killam were from Balby; John had done time in York Castle for witnessing to Truth. Gamaliel Milner was from Burton Grange, Barnsley. Anthony Pearson (1628 – 1665), of Rampshire near Bishop Auckland, was convinced while sitting as a Justice on the bench at the trial of James Nayler and Francis Howgill early in 1653; in 1657 he had published *The Great Case of Tythes*, a tract analysing the tithe-refusal issue. Thomas Taylor (*circa* 1617 – 1682) of Carleton near Skipton was Oxford-educated and an ordained priest. He was leader of a Seeker congregation, and finally became one of the Valiant Sixty; he spent long years in prison for witnessing to Truth. James Tennant of Scarhouse also owned property in Skipton. Formerly a Seeker, he was convinced with his family by George Fox in 1652. Together with three other Friends, in 1656 he was fined for refusing to take an oath of allegiance; he died in prison in York from health problems caused by long imprisonment.

In the seventeenth century, Scale House was not the large building that it is now and it is difficult to imagine how it might have accommodated a meeting of all the Friends who signed this epistle, let alone an even greater number including those who would have been present but not signed the letter. Perhaps they held their wider deliberations and meetings for worship in Airton, but withdrew to the greater comfort of Scale House for administrative business, letter writing, and small committee meetings.

1659, 2 March, at Skipton. Ten Friends attended from Yorkshire, Lancashire, Cumberland and Westmorland. This meeting offered a contribution for the needs of Friends travelling in the ministry in Ireland or Scotland, and for Friends suffering imprisonment for witnessing to the Truth. They would also have made preparations for the general meeting to be held in Skipton in June.

1659, 29 June, at Skipton. Friends were invited from the seven northern counties. Their concluding epistle, signed by 38 Friends, is again about fundraising: *We who are met together in Skipton… do see it fit and convenient that a collection be made in every particular meeting in each county for the supply of the church's several necessities, thus -- for all that are in the gaols that are not able to maintain themselves, whether for tithes or otherwise, -- and for the supply of those that go forth into the ministry into Scotland, Ireland or other places.* The epistle clarified that the cost of books and the care of the poor must be met by monthly meetings, not out of this fund. John Killam and Thomas Atkinson (probably the Thomas Atkinson of Malham who died in 1706) were present at this meeting; other local Friends were William Watkinson of Scale House and Symon Wilkinson of Bordley Maybe they had attended previous meetings, but had not felt sufficiently *weighty* to sign the previous epistles. The remaining 34 had not been at Scale House in the previous June. It is a tribute to the closeness of the Quaker community that groups with so little overlap were able to develop coherent policies. Some others who attended were: Thomas Bewley (1595 – 1680) from Caldbeck, Cumbria; Mathew Foster had been *turned out* of the Parliamentary army when he became a Quaker. Thomas Green was one of several Quakers with this name; he may have been the grocer and mercer of Lancaster who served as Friends' forwarding agent. John Moore may have been a Friend of that name from Eldroth in Craven. George Robinson of London had been in Jerusalem *under the Lord's commandment* in 1657. George Taylor (*ob.* 1696) of Kendal served Friends as financial agent to Margaret Fell. Lancelot Wardell was from Sunderland and Gateshead;.William Robinson was from Scarborough.

1659, 1 October, at Durham. This general meeting sent a letter to *Friends who shall meet together out of the several Northern Counties, at Skipton the 5th of the 8th month 1659* (the months were then counted with the year starting in March, so the eighth month would have been October). They agreed a lengthy concluding epistle with some plain speaking: *It having pleased God in these latter days to reveal the mystery of his Gospel, which hath been hid from ages and generations ... and chosen England before all other nations of the world as the land of his delight, and to bring forth many thousands therein.* They pleaded *that none may exercise lordship or dominion over another, nor the person of any be set apart but as they continue in the power of Truth.* They recommended that Friends from as many monthly meetings as convenient *in the northern parts of England... come together in a General Meeting twice or thrice in a year... and that we may not tie up ourselves to the world's limits of counties.* They laid upon *Friends in every meeting to take care of their own poor, to supply such as are aged and infirm in body, to provide employment for such as want work, and to help such parents for the education of their children as have more than they can maintain, that there may not be a beggar amongst us, nor any whose soul need be oppressed with care for food or raiment.* The epistle ended with some sound practicalities for the receipt, expenditure and accounting of money. It further advised that a General Meeting for *all England* be held annually. It seems that as of this Durham meeting in 1659, there was not yet a Yearly Meeting for *all England* but by 11 October the following year, there was, providing further evidence to consider Skipton 1660 the first Yearly Meeting. Of the 20 who signed this epistle, only Anthony Pearson had been at the Skipton/Scale House meetings. Thomas Killam, Samuel Watson and up to 25 others were also present.

1659, 5 October, at Skipton. This gathering received and approved the letter from Durham. Thomas Aldam writing to George Fox rather hastily and clumsily explained that he had been unable to attend but word of its proceedings had reached him. He knew all about the *things consented to by many Friends which met at Skipton, approved of by many who met, and things are written down which are to be done.* The written minute of the meeting recorded that the Durham letter was owned and approved by all Friends, and agreed to be observed, and that copies were to be sent to all monthly meetings. We have not found a complete attendance list, but Thomas Killam and Samuel Watson were there again, with William Gandy of Cheshire, who had been at Scale House in June 1658, and Henry Ward of Grayrigg north-east of Kendal. Friends travelling in the ministry were frequently entertained in their home by Henry and his wife; in 1656 he travelled with George Fox in Cornwall. An Epistle from this meeting was signed by 18 Friends.

1660, Wednesday 25 April, at Skipton. This was the culmination and maybe the last of the series of meetings at Scale House and Skipton. Friends may have met at the edge of Skipton on the town green by Schoolhouse Beck, perhaps on the land where Skipton meeting house was built 33 years later. This meeting is now accounted the first yearly meeting of the Society of Friends in Britain. Its epistle was signed by 42 Friends. It concerns itself with travelling ministry *in the service to the Truth* throughout America, Europe, India and the Middle East. Fundraising is recommended *that every particular meeting in every county may do herein as they are moved thereunto by the Lord.... For England is as a family of prophets, which must spread over all nations as a garden of plants, and the place where the pearl is found which must enrich all nations with the heavenly treasure, out of which shall the waters of life flow, and water all the thirsty ground....* Dictating his Journal 15 years later, George Fox well remembered this meeting and his journey to it: *I passed to Balby where was our yearly meeting and many thousands of people and Friends was gathered there and met in John Killam's orchard.... And the next day we had a heavenly meeting in Warmsworth of Friends in the ministry.... And from Warmsworth aforesaid in the Lord's power I passed through the country to Burton* [Bolton] *Abbey where I had a great meeting, and from thence to Thos. Taylor's* [at Carleton] *and from thence to Skipton where there was a general meeting of men Friends out of many counties concerning the affairs of the church.... some Friends did come out of most parts of this nation and beyond the seas. For when I was in the North several years before I was moved to set up that meeting....*

The town's overseers of the poor and its constables came to break up this gathering of strangers, whom they regarded as vagrants who might become chargeable on the parish. When Friends demonstrated from their records and account books how they took care of their needy members, so that none became a charge on the rates, the parish officers' hostility turned to friendship. George Fox recalled that *they passed away lovingly and commended Friends' practice.* He further recalls: *And many times* [at Skipton] *there would be two hundred beggars of the world there (for all the country knew we met about the poor), which after the meeting was done Friends would send to the bakers and give them a penny loaf apiece be them as many as would.* In Fox's description of these meetings, we see a distinction between: the great concourse at Balby open to thousands of people for worship and for hearing inspirational ministry, the meeting of travelling ministers held at Warmsworth, and the meeting held at Skipton to attend to business and church affairs *in this nation and beyond the seas.*

1660, 11 October, Skipton. This general meeting of Elders from the six northern counties was about money *collected and disbursed for the general service of the Truth....* [T]*he substantial men and Elders in the Truth came to the Yearly Meeting at Skipton, both from Bristol and London, and other places; and there they gave an account of the prosperity and the spreading of the Lord's blessed Truth, and of what Friends the Lord moved to go beyond the seas: for all that (in the motion of the Lord) did travel into any parts or beyond the seas, they made the Monthly, Quarterly, or Yearly Meetings acquainted.... And all these meetings looked to see that all walked according to the Gospel of Christ, and were faithful, and that all the poor in all the counties were looked after. And then the Yearly Meeting was removed to John Crook's* [in Bedfordshire].... *And after, the Yearly Meeting was kept at Balby in Yorkshire where there was many thousands of people, and likewise at Skipton the same year by the Elders there ordered from all parts, in the year 1660. And from thence it was removed to London the next year, where it hath been kept ever since, as being looked upon a more convenient place....* This meeting appointed a further general meeting to be held on the **7th March at Skipton** though no evidence has been found that it took place.

1661, 1st November at Kendal . A general meeting of Friends from Cheshire, Lancashire, Yorkshire, Westmorland, Cumberland, Durham; Scale House's George and William Watkinson were present.

Friends who attended general meetings at Skipton or Scale House (?Airton) in 1658-1660 To find who attended these meetings and what they did I [Richard Harland] have looked at: contemporary letters in Friends House Library; what George Fox put in his Journal about fifteen years later and in his memorandum thirty years later, with Norman Penney's notes to his Cambridge edition (1911) of the Journal; Ernest E Taylor, *The Valiant Sixty* (1947) (indicated by [VS] in the table below); and A. R. Barclay (ed.), *Letters etc. of Early Friends* (1841) and *Epistles ... 1681-1857* (1858), vol. I, xxix. The Friends House Library has seventeenth-century copies of early letters and epistles with additional names to those listed in published editions of the letters; Friends whose names appear in these are marked with an asterisk in the list below. All who signed the epistles are men; 105 signed at least once. George Fox is among those who came to these meetings, but did not sign the epistles. There was much more to talk of than went into the public letters. Those who came to the regional and yearly meetings were, in my [Richard Harland's] phrase, enablers of *the Truth*, a largely different set from the *Valiant Sixty,* men and women who travelled as publishers or preachers of *the Truth*. To gather details of this group of 105 men of strong character would build a picture of one aspect of the Quaker community in the North in its first decade. The list would be enriched by seeing them alongside the *Valiant Sixty,* who were also mostly northerners; only seven men figure in both groups. Six Friends signed the epistle from Durham on the first of October and also that from Skipton on the fifth of October or from another of our meetings; those present at Durham who signed none of the Scale House or Skipton epistles are not listed here. Men who signed epistles sent from or are otherwise identified as having attended one of the meetings held at Scale House, at Skipton and the one at Durham are listed alphabetically in the table below. Others who would have been present, but who did not sign any epistle and who were not mentioned in any other letters or documents are not listed.

	24.6.1658 Scale House	29.6.1659 Skipton	1.10.1659 Durham	5.10.1659 Skipton	25.4.1660 Skipton
Thomas Aldam [vs] *c.*1616 – 1660 of Warmsworth	x				x
Edward Allcock		x			
Oliver Atherton *ob.* 1663 of Ormskirk	x				
Thomas Atkinson *c.*1604 – 1684 of Cartmel	x	x			
John Baldwin		x			
John Bancroft					x
Marmaduke Beckwith		x			
Gervase Benson [vs] also signed letter on 11.3.58	x				
Thomas Bewley *c.*1595 – 1680 of Caldbeck	x	x			x
Robert Boulton					x
Thomas Brocksop	x				
James Browne *ob.* 1666/7 of Frodsham, Cheshire				x	
Robert Bulcocke	x	x			x
Robert Burrett					x
Joseph Camplin		x			
William Cartmell				x	
Peter Crosby	x				
Richard Davis					x
Henry Dickinson		x			
George Ellis		x			
Joseph Endon	x				
John Fallowfield	x	x			
Thomas Farnsworth (Farneworth) *ob.* 1666	x				

of Tickhill					
Richard Fletcher ? from nr Carslile	x				
Matthew Foster		x			
George Fox [vs] 1624 – 1691					x
William Gandy *ob.* 1683 of Frandley, Cheshire	x			x	x
Thomas Goodaire [vs] *ob.* 1693, of Selby signed letter on 11.3.1658 from Scale House					
Robert Goslinge ? of Richmond	x				
Thomas Greene 1628 – 1703 of Lancaster		x			
John Grime					x
William Handy	x				
Peter Hardcastle		x			
Richard Hargreaves					x
Roger Harper	x				
John Hodgson	x				
Cuthbert Hodgson				x	
John Hogg		x			
John Hooper ?of Co. Durham		x			
William Horner		x			
Richard Hunter	x				
William Hurst (or Hairst)		x		x	x
Christopher Hutton					x
John Killam of Balby	x	x	x	x	
Thomas Killam [vs] *ob.* 1690 of Balby	x	x	x		
Thomas Lawson [vs] 1630 – 1691, of Great Strickland	see note below				
Thomas Lawson [vs] *ob.* 1679 of Borrat near Sedbergh	see note below				
Robert Macfoerth		x			

Gamaliel Milner of Barnsley	x				
Gregory Milner	x				
John Moor *c.1630 – c.1690* of Eldroth, Settle		x			
Christopher Moore		x			
John Nixon				x	
John Paddifield	x				
Anthony Patrickson	x				
Anthony Pearson *c.1628 – 1665* of Co. Durham	x		x	x	
Thomas Pearson of Westmorland	x	x			
Robert Porrett					x
George Preston of Holker, nr Cartmel				x	
John Radcliff	x				
Andrew Raw	x		x	x	
John Rawson		x			
John Richardson of Darlington	x				
Martin Richmond of Co. Durham					x
Gerrard Roberts c.1621-1703 of London					x
Anthony Robinson		x			
George Robinson ?of London		x			x
John Robinson [a]	x				
John Robinson [b]	x	x			
John Robinson [c]	x				
Mathew Robinson *ob.* 1697 of Greysouthen, nr. Cockermouth				x	
Thomas Robinson		x			
William Robinson ? of Scarborough		x			
Thomas Rowley	x				
Thomas Samson	x				
Thomas Sawley		x			
William Sawley		x			
Richard Smithe		x			
William Smith ? ob. 1672, ? of Besthorpe, Notts	x				

Francis Smithson	x				
Thomas Stangg	x				
Amor Stoddart *ob.* 1670, of Notts & London					x
Marmaduke Storr *ob.* 1678, of Ostwick in Holderness	x				x
Thomas Stubbs *ob.* 1673 of Dalston, Cumberland	x				
Phillip Swale of Swaledale	x			x	
George Taylor *ob.* 1696 of Kendal	x	x		x	
Thomas Taylor [vs], *c.*1617-1682 of Carleton, Skipton	x				
James Tennant of Hubberholm, Wharfedale	x				
Edward Thompson				x	
Thomas Thomson	x				
Hugh Tickill (or Tickell) *c.*1610 – 1680 of Portinscale	x				x
John Tiffin		x			
George Troter				x	
Richard Wallace from nr. Stockport	x				
Richard Wallne ? of Bowland	x				
Charles Walmsley		x			
Henry Ward *ob.* 1674 of Grayrigg			x	x	
Lancelot Wardell of Sunderland or Gateshead		x	x		
George Watkinson *ob.* 1670 of Scotton, nr. Knaresborough					x
William Watkinson,		x			

of Rylstone, nr. Airton				
Samuel Watson c.1618 – 1708 of Stainforth. nr. Settle	x		x		x
Robert Wharton					x
Thomas Wigglesworth		x			
Simeon Wilkinson of Bordley, nr Airton		x			

A few additional details can be added to some of the names in the above table. Richard Harland's notes do not specify which of the several General and Yearly Meetings either of the Thomas Lawsons attended. Gervase Benson is mentioned in several contexts above. Thomas Brocksopp was perhaps related to Joan Brocksopp, who took *the Truth* to New England in 1661. Richard Davis was one of the *dear brethern from London* to whom was committed money collected in the North for Friends' work abroad. Was he the man with whom George Fox fell out in 1658? Matthew Foster was one of the Quakers ejected from the army in 1657. A large Quaker meeting was held at William Gandy's in 1657: *we came... to Will. Gandys &... had a meeting of about 2 or 3 thousand people.* Robert Goslinge is mentioned in Besse as one who was informed against. The Thomas Greene who attended the Skipton meeting is most likely from Lancaster; another Quaker Thomas Green (1633-99) lived in London. John Killam, brother-in-law of Thomas Aldam, was imprisoned in York Castle in 1654-55. He attended the 1659 meeting in Durham and the 1661 meeting in Kendal; *many thousands* met in his orchard in 1660. Thomas Killam, brother of John, was also a brother-in-law of Thomas Aldam; he travelled much in the ministry. Most probably he attended the meeting held in Skipton on the 13th of March. John Moore, of Eldroth, married the sister of Samuel Watson, of Stainforth. Martin Richard, of County Durham, was convinced to join Friends at Anthony Pearson's house, also in County Durham.

8.   William and Alice Ellis

William Ellis's father, Stephen Ellis, was a hand-loom linen weaver living in Calton. He would have been a contemporary of the tailor John Hall, perhaps supplying him with some of the cloth that was made into clothing for the Lambert family of Calton Hall. William (1658-1709), who was christened in Kirkby Malham church, was in 1674 apprenticed to John Stott, a Quaker linen weaver in Skipton. Perhaps the apprenticeship was recommended or facilitated by John Hall, who was by then an influential Quaker who had formerly lived in Airton. In 1676, Roger Haydock, of Penrith, together with his future wife, Eleanor Love, and her cousin, Elizabeth Hodson, ministered at a Quaker meeting in Lower Bradley, about two miles southwest of Skipton; Ellis attended this meeting. Convinced by the preaching he heard of the rightness of Quaker teaching, he joined with Friends, and was soon recognised as having a gift of spoken ministry. In 1679, he moved to Airton, where he built a house and a hand-loom workshop on land between the Lambert's dower house and the Airton Meeting House, which was directly across the road. (Airton Mill was then a small water-powered corn mill.) William was a master weaver whose business so prospered that he was able to employ *a considerable number* of young men. Excavation for an interment in the Airton burial ground in 2014 recovered a roughly-shaped sandstone disc, about three inches in diameter and almost a half inch thick. Such discs were used on some small looms in the seventeenth century in lieu of a warp beam or wooden bobbin to hold the individual warp threads. This example provides a tangible link to the industrious profession of William Ellis and his employees.

Starting in 1686, two years before William Ellis's marriage to Alice Davies, he travelled at his own expense as a ministering Friend. He was in East Yorkshire in 1686, in the south of England in about 1690, and in Ireland in 1694. Settle Monthly Meeting wrote a travelling minute [letter of introduction] dated *5th of 10th month* 1694, to support William in his proposed travels in Ireland. *William Ellis, a friend and member of our meeting, unto whom the Lord hath committed a gift in the ministry of the word of Life and sent him forth many, or several times in his work and service,..... to visit the meetings of Friends in Ireland.... he hath ordered and disposed of his outward concerns to the care and comfort of this wife, and his wife's willingness and freeness to give him up to that service.... [we] commend him unto you to receive him as a brother in the Truth....* This minute was signed on behalf of Settle Monthly Meeting by John Tatham. In 1698 William Ellis was in correspondence with John's brother, James Tatham. Another John Tatham, a descendant of the one who signed the minute quoted above, was the Clerk of Settle Monthly Meeting in 1849; he drew a frontispiece illustration of Airton Meeting House that was published by Backhouse (1849). In 2004, Rachel Cundall of Newcastle-upon-Tyne sent Richard Harland a photocopy of the original document quoted above and said that she had been brought up as a Quaker in Settle, where her father and grandfather (surname Horner) had been photographers and that John Tatham, who signed the minute for Ellis on behalf of Settle Monthly Meeting was their ancestor.

In two letters sent from Ireland to his wife in Airton, one on the *26th of the 11th month* 1694 and one on the *30th of the 1st month* 1695, William Ellis asked to be remembered to many local Friends, to whom he sent greetings: Richard Wilkinson and his family, Thomas Stockdale and his wife and family, old Phineas Parkinson, William Hartley, Francis Atkinson, George Leemin, sister Jennet Davy, Jennet Stall, and Abigail Stott; in one letter he asked to be remembered to *all my servants* in the other he wrote of *all my men.* He enquired after James Conyers, who had *an unruly spirit*, and had special messages for two others: *and to Daniel, bid him to order his affairs so that you may have his company at week-day meetings .... Bid Solomon love the God of his father, and of his father's servant* (Backhouse 1849, pp. 11 and 17-18).

In a letter written to an unidentified recipient on the *24ᵗʰ of the 6ᵗʰ month* 1697, William Ellis said, *I gave you a hint before, how I got up a meeting house; but now shall give a small account of the good service we have had since we got it in order. Many public-friends come to us and great numbers of people at times; and the Lord's goodness opens wonderfully, so that people declare their satisfaction one to another; so that I am in great hopes, great part of our valley will be convinced...* (Backhouse 1849, pp. 32-34). This work would not have been done in 1697 while William was preparing to travel to North America. Had it been completed shortly before the date of the letter, it would have been fresh in his mind and he would have named an approximate date or said something like *last year* or *two years ago*. This makes a date of 1693 or 1694 most probable, and such a date accords well with the architectural evidence for the age of the Meeting House's oak panels and partition wall. What was the work that the Ellises had done? Clearly, it was not to build the Airton Meeting House; had they done that, William would have said so. Rather, they refurbished, repaired and furnished the existing Meeting House, that is the indisputable meaning of the redundant phrases *got up a meeting house* and *got it in order*. The *great numbers of people* who sometimes attended these meetings could not have been accommodated in the Ellis's family home. Two letters, written on the 16ᵗʰ and the 24ᵗʰ of the *5ᵗʰ month* 1697 and sent from London are interesting. *To Simeon Wilkinson, with the rest of my servants.... it is now your day as to the great kindness of God, and as to liberty to go to meetings.... Pray consider the reason why there are so many that fall asleep when met together to worship God,....* This mention of *liberty to go to meetings* may be a subtle reference to the 1689 Act of Toleration, which allowed Dissenters to attend licensed meeting houses without fear of persecution for doing so. The second letter is to John Tomlinson, *concerning Friends of our own meeting.... thou art one whom we thought most fit to be joined with the other two Friends as overseers.... watch to keep all disorders from amongst you.... it hath been my concern for many years....* These letters would have been written while William was preparing to visit North America, a voyage from which it was possible he might not return (Backhouse, 1849 pp. 29-31). While it is possible that some aspect of the Penn – Lambert – Blackwell connection may have influenced William's decision to travel in the New World in general or to Pennsylvania and the Jerseys in particular, there is no mention in his correspondence of such a link. In 1700, York Quarterly Meeting gave James Conyers of Rylstone a grant to assist with his emigration; it is not unlikely that his decision to move to North America was influenced by William's reports of life there.

According to Settle Meeting's memorial testimony to William Ellis, *it pleased the Lord to Concern him to visit Peoples of God in foreign Countries... having the concurrence of his Friends and Bretheren along with him therein: At length he did set forward on his Journey, and Voyage for America, leaving his Wife and Family in the Ninth Month 1697. And took Shipping at Deal in Kent, in the tenth month... arriving on the Fourteenth Day of the First Month following, in Maryland.... he arriving again in England, the Twenty-third of the Fourth Month, 1699* (York Quarterly Meeting 1710, p.11; Backhouse 1849, pp. 260-261). Over the course of about one-and-a-half years, William held meetings and travelled in Carolina, Virginia, Maryland, Pennsylvania, East and West Jersey, Long Island and Rhode Island. Subsequent to his safe return, he maintained an active correspondence with Friends in all the places he had visited. One of the many travelling Friends who stayed with the Ellises in Airton was Samuel Bownas, who said William was *a great, good man full of power, having great and solid experience concerning the ministry. His words were like "apples of gold in pictures of silver"; for a long time after the sense and virtue of them stayed on my mind, to my great advantage.* Thomas Thomson wrote of William that, *In the Year 1686, it was his Lot to visit Friends Meetings in the East-part of Yorkshire.... From that time I became acquainted with him, and found him to be more in the Root, than in Appearance; his Company was pleasant, his Conversation easie and delightful; a great lover of Unity and Concord he was, and laboured greatly to promote the Same among Bretheren; his Concern was great, for the increase of the Government of Christ, and for the promotion of good Order and Discipline in the Church...* (York Quarterly Meeting, 1710 pp 11-12). The last occasion on which William spoke in public ministry was at a Yearly Meeting held in Lancaster in February 1709. John Kelsall, a Welsh schoolmaster recorded the occasion: *the public meetings were attended by a very great number of Friends.... Amongst other brethren, our dear friend, William Ellis, had a blessed opportunity, and was carried on in the power of life and Truth, even beyond a usual manner.... he being full of love, full of zeal, full of courage, and as one triumphant over the devil and the powers of darkness, and in the divine regions of light and life. This was indeed a glorious season... so that many were made to say afterwards that they had not known the like. And in this exaltation of life and power, the meeting concluded.* Others of his contemporaries spoke of his kindness, good humour and generosity. *Although he had little or nothing from his father, he being but of low circumstances in the world, yet he soon began to be helpful in the Church, by distributing towards the relief of the poor, out of what he got by hard labour and great diligence and industry in his calling.... He freely gave up a great deal of his time to attend meetings, not only such as were for public worship, but also meetings for business and the affairs of the church.... it pleased God to bless his endeavours with success, so that his outward substance increased; and as that was enlarged, so his heart opened, and he gladly made use of opportunities in which he might lay out a great part thereof in the service of Truth* (Backhouse 1849, pp. 245-246). His was a major influence in helping the Religious Society of Friends in Britain and in the New World to mature from their sometimes turbulent beginnings.

A list of the 27 Friends, all men, who signed Settle Monthly Meeting's testimony to William Ellis is of some interest.

Isaac Armistead	John Moore, snr
John Armistead, jnr	John Rawson
John Armistead, snr	Thomas Rud
William Armistead	William Slater
John Atkinson	Adam Squire
William Berkbeck	William Stockdale
John Buttershire	John Tomlinson
Thomas Carr	Robert Tunstall
Richard Clough	John Weatheralt
Joseph Hall	Thomas Wilde
William Holt	Richard Wilkinson
John King	Simeon Wilkinson
Laurence King	William Windle
John Moore, jnr	

Alice Ellis, whose maiden name was Davy or Davies, died in 1720. Although her date and place of birth are unrecorded, she may have been a member of the Davies family of Whitley Head, who were active seventeenth-century Quakers in the Keighley area (Baumber, *circa.* 1975). She and William could have met while he was an apprentice in Skipton, as the

Stott family by whom he was employed and the Davies are likely to have visited one another from time to time, whether while attending Quaker meetings or the Skipton markets. Starting soon after their marriage, Alice managed the weaving business during William's absences when he travelled as a Quaker minister. Their only child, a son born in 1692, lived for just one year. Thereafter, both she and her husband devoted much of their efforts and income to working for Friends. In addition to supervising the weaving business while William was abroad, Alice welcomed visiting Friends and travelling ministers to their home and sometimes spoke as a minister in meetings for worship. Her testimony memorialising her husband reflects much on herself: *He was a loving husband and in great unity and Fellowship we lived together... I had great unity with his Travels in Truths service.... He was also a kind Friend and a good Neighbour, delighting to do good unto all....* (York Quarterly Meeting, 1710 p.6). She was an active participant in the regional conduct of Friends' organisational affairs and was especially supportive of Quaker women's involvement in church governance. A testimony to Alice Ellis, written by Settle Friends, speaks of her *great love to, and zeal for, the promotion of blessed, holy Truth... by her conversation amongst us, her friends, and also amongst people of other persuasions.... She was a very constant attender of First-day and week-day meetings, at the meeting places she belonged to; and also accompanied travelling Friends very often to neighbouring meetings.... and sometimes she appeared in public testimony.... She was also a very constant attender of meetings for the business and affairs of the church... and was a diligent attender of Quarterly Meetings also.... She had a tender regard to the poor amongst all sorts of people... she being particularly devoted to acts of hospitality...* (Backhouse 1849, pp. 271-274). The cumbersome phrase *the meeting places she belonged to* seems to be a circumlocution to avoid mentioning Airton Meeting and Meeting House, which both she and William so very largely supported.

It may have been Alice Ellis who devised the partition screen with hanging shutters in our Meeting House so that women Friends could have a separate space in which to hold business meetings to consider those matters with which they were most closely concerned, including care of the needy and the education of children. Similar screens are an eighteenth-century feature of Skipton, Settle and several other Quaker meeting houses further afield. The Airton screen, which predates these, could have been their prototype. In 1710, the year after William's death, Alice had much work done to the Meeting House property including enlarging the ancillary structure at its west end which had originally been a very small cottage, but by then served as a stable, and rebuilding it as a two-storey cottage, now called The Nook. She had a large new stable and hayloft constructed as a detached building at right angles to the Meeting House and cottage. She also had the Meeting House's seating capacity and comfort increased by raising its roof to match that of the adjacent cottage, building a gallery above the smaller meeting room, inserting two new fireplaces and enlarging the Meeting House's south-facing windows. In 1720, her will confirmed the gift to Quaker trustees of the Meeting House and its adjoining cottage, the stables and the burial ground which she and William had endowed in 1706 and added to their original bequest 29 acres of land in the township of Airton, turbary on the moors, and also the Ellises' own house, workshops and another cottage opposite the Meeting House. Income from letting these properties was to be used to provide hospitality for travelling Quaker ministers, apprenticeships for Quaker children and for the children of families living in Airton, and cloaks to be lent to men and women Friends travelling to and from Airton.

Usually, Quaker testimonies memorialising deceased Friends mention the particular or local meeting to which they belonged, however, it is notable that neither the Settle

Monthly Meeting testimony to Alice nor those of Settle Monthly Meeting and York Quarterly Meeting in remembrance of William Ellis include any mention of Airton Meeting and Meeting House, which they both so actively supported. Nothing is recorded of its purchase and endowment to Friends, nor of Alice's charitable endowment of their own house, fields and grazing rights lands in and near Airton.

9.   The Eighteenth and Nineteenth Centuries

On the 24th of June 1697, John Lambert, the son of Major General John Lambert, granted to William Ellis for 1,000 years, for an initial consideration of £200 and a yearly rent of one penny, *All that parte and so much of that garth or garden intake in the said Ayrton at a place called stable gate and adjoining on the highway over against the said William Ellis's new dwelling house and in the whole containing eight falls, poles or perches after the rate of seven yards to the pole or perch....* This was for land adjoining what is now called Ellis House, opposite Airton Meeting House on the north side of the road. Three years later, on the 30th March 1700, he granted to William Ellis for 5,000 years at a yearly rent of three pence and an initial consideration of £31 *All that one parcel of arable or meadow ground commonly called The Croft containing by estimation half an acre be the same more or lesse and all that one house, barn or stable situate, standing and being on that part of the said parcel of ground which doth adjoyne to the Common Street in the said Ayrton.....* This comprised the walled burial ground with some additional land and the Airton Meeting House, which had recently been refurbished by the Ellises, together with an ancillary structure on the western end of the Meeting House. The latter may originally have been part of the ancient field barn which was precursor to the Meeting House. When the Meeting House was built, in about 1610, this annex became a one- or two-room cottage with an external door and window in its south wall, facing the cut-away hillside. By 1710, it seems to have been used as a stable. By that date, the Meeting House had served as such for approximately a century. Attention may be called to the very different terms of these two long leases. That for the land on the north side of the road, on which the Ellis house and workshop were built, was for a plot of approximately a quarter of an acre. That for the Meeting House and burial ground was for a plot of approximately a half an acre. The former lease cost £200 for 1,000 years; the latter cost £31 for 5,000 years. Unless there were genuine differences in the values of these two plots of land or other factors of which we are unaware, it seems that very favourable terms were given for purchase of the Meeting House and burial ground. This suggests that the fourth John Lambert may have been as sympathetic to and as willing to shelter and encourage Friends meetings as was his more famous father. In 1706 and subsequently confirmed in Alice's will, the Ellises endowed the Meeting House, associated buildings and burial ground to Quaker trustees together with their home across the road, fields in Airton, and moorland grazing rights, all of which were intended to maintain the Meeting House, provide hospitality for visiting Friends, support poor Friends and pay apprenticeship fees for the children of Quakers and for the poor of Airton. Alice also instructed that *six men's coats and six women's hoods which had been kept for the use of travelling Friends ... should be kept for the same use.* Among others, Josiah Box was apprenticed in 1712 to Simeon Wilkinson, linen weaver of Otterburn, Aaron Sheppard was apprenticed to John Rawson, a linen and woollen weaver of Airton, and Christopher Hall, son of Joseph Hall of Airton was apprenticed with the help of this fund. Simeon Wilkinson and John Rawson were former employees of William Ellis.

That the increased seating capacity provided by raising the roof and inserting a gallery in the Meeting House and new stabling were wanted for those attending Quaker meetings in Airton and that a new Quaker meeting house was built between Rylstone and Hetton in 1711 suggests that in the early decades of the eighteenth century there were large attendances at Quaker meetings in the Malhamdale-Wharfedale area. William Ellis had reported that *great numbers* attended Quaker meeting in Airton in the 1690s. Airton Meeting House saw at least two phases of improvements in the eighteenth century, once in 1710 when the stables and hayloft that are now called The Barn were built to accommodate the horses of those who rode to meetings, and again later in the same century when oak wainscoting was removed from the side walls of the main meeting room and reused to front the gallery railing and a new pine facing bench was installed. (The large window in the Meeting House's north wall was installed much later, probably at the end of the nineteenth century.) These refurbishments indicate that Quakerism flourished locally well into the eighteenth century. However, this situation did not last. Both locally and nationally, in the first half of the eighteenth century Quakerism began to diminish as some whose ancestors had been of more radical inclination emigrated abroad, moved from rural to urban employment, or joined one of the larger and more formal churches. In 1743, it was reported to Archbishop Hering that at Airton *we have 230 families of which 6 only are Quakers.... the Quakers have a meeting house where they meet to the number of about 20 on Sundays and Wednesdays.* Although the eighteenth-century parish-by-parish reports of dissenter activities frequently underestimated their numbers (Phillipson, 1998), this attendance is nowhere near the *great numbers* that William Ellis reported as attending Quaker meetings in Airton fifty years previously. The decline in Quaker numbers was not just a local phenomenon. Between the late seventeenth and the mid-nineteenth centuries, it is estimated that the number of Friends nationally fell from approximately 50,000 to about 14,000 (Rubenstein, 2005).

In 1773 James Backhouse had a map engraved for the use of Friends travelling in the ministry in West Yorkshire, showing the distances between then-active Quaker meetings and meeting houses. This places Airton at a crossroad with branches leading to Skipton (10 miles), Settle (6 miles), Lothersdale/Salterforth (10 miles), and Starbotton (11 miles). By the middle of the eighteenth century, it was recognised by the Yorkshire Quarterly Meeting that as small rural meetings shrank and those attending them aged, they were becoming isolated from the events and concerns of Friends regionally and nationally. In 1784, a Quarterly Meeting committee was delegated to ensure that reputable and worthy Quakers, sometimes referred to as *weighty* Friends, visited regularly the meetings in Rylstone, Newton in Bowland, and Airton. The visitors, who came to each of these small meetings once a quarter, were tasked with offering spiritual support and pastoral care, which would have taken the form of attendance at meetings for worship and home visits (Wright, 2006 p. 19). If one of the visitors was a recognised Quaker minister, it might be anticipated that he or she would preach at some length and sometimes a larger group of non-Quakers would come to hear what was said. This intervention, which continued at least intermittently for the next 60 years, helped to keep Airton Meeting alive, but was not sufficient to prevent its further decline. The Yorkshire Quarterly Meeting minutes for July 1796 record of Airton that, *only two men and two women in membership, two of these through indisposition and infirmity, together with the distance of 10 miles do not attend.... there are several others who are not Members who attend particularly on 1st days.* Four years later, in 1800, there was a consideration of whether Airton Meeting should be closed. This suggestion was not acted upon and the Airton Meeting House remained in use throughout the nineteenth century. With the purchase of Airton Mill by John Greenwood in 1819, and the purchase of its lease in 1825 and its freehold in 1834 by John Dewhurst, who converted the mill to cotton spinning, the population of Airton increased from 139 in 1801 to 225 in 1851 and stayed at about that level for the remainder of the nineteenth century. Consequently, the number of Friends attending Airton Meeting increased. In 1822, the Settle Monthly Meeting minutes record that Airton Meeting was *satisfactorily kept up.* There are hearsay accounts that sometimes as many as 200 people attended Quaker meetings, and even larger numbers the Methodist Chapel in Airton. Between 1813 and 1837, the whole of Settle Monthly Meeting decreased from 142 to just 84 members. Writing in 1849, James Backhouse says, *The present tenant of the house at Airton, formerly occupied by William and Alice Ellis, is John Shakelton, a Friend who, with his family, gladly carries out the design of the original occupants, in the hospitable entertainment of ministers and other Friends.... A small congregation now assembles in the meeting house at Airton, in which also Settle Monthly Meeting is held in the Fifth and Tenth months.... the five meetings of Settle, Bentham, Newton in Bowland, Lothersdale and Airton of which the Monthly Meeting is composed are all very small.*

Airton Meeting House together with its associated buildings and burial grounds is depicted on the Ordinance Survey maps for 1853 and 1892. On both of these, the area of the original burial ground is demarcated by a wall running approximately east-west across the northernmost portion of the walled grounds. This wall, which appears to be of the same age as the original construction of the Meeting House, is also shown in the engraving of a drawing by Thomas Tatham of Settle Meeting which was published in 1849 as a frontispiece to James Backhouse's *Life and Correspondence of William and Alice Ellis of Airton*. It and the Meeting House itself are shown in the engraving as being in good repair and the grassed yard well maintained; only a stump of that wall now remains. The maps of 1853 and 1892 each show The Barn extended northwards to abut The Nook, as it does today, and a small annex or outbuilding on the south gable end of The Barn. That annex no longer exists. Probably these enlargements of The Barn were made early in the nineteenth century. In the second half of the nineteenth century, the upper floor of the Airton Barn was sometimes used as a place where travelling peddlers exhibited their wares. According to the unpublished memoirs of Arnold Waterfall, a copy of which is in the Malhamdale Local History Group archives, the room then became known as *The Klondyke* on account of the treasures which might be found for sale. With closure in 1904 of the cotton mill, which had been a significant local employer, the population of Airton and attendance at Quaker meetings again declined. Of the Quaker meetings in our immediate area that had been active in the seventeenth and eighteenth centuries, those at Scarhouse, Arncliffe, Litton, Starbotton, Bolton, Addingham (Farfield), Scale House, Hetton, Rylstone, and Flasby were closed and largely forgotten by the end of the nineteenth. Friends no longer met regularly in Skipton, though they continued to own the Skipton Meeting House. In 1814, Settle (local) Meeting had so few members it was unable to appoint either a Clerk or an Overseer. Writing in 1882, Dawson (pp 303-304) says that, *Quakerism is now nearly extinct in Skipton. After the death of Mr. Hodgson, who was Castle Steward, the interest began to wane, and when the Smith and Binns families died out or removed from the locality few were left to carry on the cause. Meetings are now very seldom held....* By the end of the century, both Skipton and Settle Meetings were closed for a number of years. Although Quaker meetings in Airton were scarcely better attended, they did continue. It was then and is now one of only a few remaining rural meetings in Yorkshire. Rylstone Meeting had ceased in 1792, was declared inoperative in 1809; its building and burial ground were sold in 1813. Its building was subsequently used for many years as a barn. but is now a private house with a garden encompassing the former burial ground. A fireplace in this house is almost identical to those which Alice Ellis had installed in the Airton Meeting House in 1710. As the following table shows, the numbers recorded as attending Sunday morning meetings for worship at each of the still-operative Friends meeting houses in our area on particular dates were low.

	AIRTON	FARFIELD	KEIGHLEY	SETTLE	SKIPTON
30th March 1851	8	12	10	7	24
Unspecified date November 1904	7	36	11	17	0

Not only Quakers were few in number in early modern Skipton; in 1774, the only places of worship in Skipton were the parish church and the Friends Meeting House. Although there had been Congregationalist preaching in the town as early as 1650, this soon died away. Renewed attempts resulted in the establishment of a Congregationalist Sunday school with 83 members in 1833. John Wesley visited Skipton in 1764 and again in 1766, but by 1769 Skipton had disappeared from mention in the Methodist circuit books until it was re-established in 1787. A small Methodist chapel was built in 1791, enlarged in 1811, and a new chapel built in 1861. A Primitive Methodist chapel was built in 1835; in 1837 its Sunday school was attended by 87 boys and 83 girls, but by 1844 their numbers had almost halved. In the early 19th century, the parish of Skipton had about 6,200 inhabitants, somewhat over 4,000 of whom lived in Skipton town. People living in the eastern parts of the geographically large parish could attend services in the Established Church at Bolton Abbey. Skipton residents were accommodated by the parish church on the top of the High Street, next to Skipton Castle, which had seating for up to 900 adults. Not until 1839 was a second Established Church provided in Skipton, with seating for up to 630 people. From these figures, it is apparent that participation in religions services was not a primary concern of many Skipton residents. The same was undoubtedly true in Malhamdale and in all the smaller villages and rural areas of Craven. A survey made on the 30th March 1851 reported that Skipton had five places for public worship, capable of accommodating a total of 1,374 people, but that only 246 attended public services in the morning and 200 in the evening.

Sometime in the early- or mid-twentieth century, books which had constituted the Airton Meeting House library were transferred to Skipton Meeting House and subsequently donated to the J.B. Priestley Library at Bradford University, to comprise a special collection of Airton books. Richard Harland's list of these and their annotations is copied here. Their publication dates, ranging from 1723 to early in the twentieth century, give a glimpse into the concerns and interests of nineteenth-century Friends; the names of donors and inscriptions on some flyleaves are also of interest. In addition to the titles listed below, a copy of *A Guide to True Peace*, published in 1813 and inscribed *Agnes Shackleton Jr. 1814 Airton 8 mo 30* was given to Craven Museum in 1972. *Piety Promoted*, of which the library included seven copies, is a selection of brief biographies of prominent Quakers. With the exception of two anti-war titles, and Besse's large, but by no means exhaustive, compilation of the persecutions, distraints, imprisonments and other sufferings of early Friends, all of the books in Airton Meeting's library were biographies, autobiographies and memoirs of eminent Quakers, whose lives and spiritual travails were thought worthy of emulation.

title	publication date	donor or inscription
Piety Promoted	preface dated 1723	George Cartwright of Airton
Piety Promoted (3 copies)	preface dated 1789	one donated by John Cowgill
Piety Promoted	preface dated 1811	John Shackleton 1853
Piety Promoted	preface dated 1829	
Piety Promoted	preface dated 1912	
Journal of John Woolman	1840	Elizabeth Bilton, Huddersfield 1854
Extracts from Approved Documents	1837	Sarah Tatham, Settle
Autobiographical Narrations of S. Crisp & 4 others	1848	1884 inscription
Memoirs of William Foster	1865	
Extracts from the letters of Jonathan Hutchinson	1841	Sarah Tatham, Settle 1841
Lives of Samuel and Mary Neale	1845	Sarah Tatham, Settle 1845
A Memoir of Mary Capper	1847	presented to Airton Meeting by Catherine Backhouse 1852
Life & Gospels of Stephen Grellet by B. Seebhom	1860	J. & S. Cowgill 1860
Journal of the Life and Gospel Labrus Life of Pike & Oxley	1837	Sarah Tatham 1838
All War Anti-Christian	1844	This book belongs to the Friends of Airton Particular Meeting
War from a Quaker Point of View by J. Graham	early 20th century	
Journal of David Sands	1848	
Journal of George Richardus	1804	
Memoirs of Stephen Crisp	1824	
Life of W. Dewsbury	1836	
Memoir of Maria Fox	1846	
Journal of Wm Caton & J. W. Yeats	1839	
Besse's Sufferings	(7 copies, publication dates not noted)	

10. The Twentieth Century

In the summer of 1905 a group of Young Friends intent on reviving small and dormant Quaker meetings and on fostering the Adult School movement visited Airton. Writing in *The Friend* of the 6th October 1905, they describe how they *met at Skipton, on Wednesday afternoon .... We lost no time in visiting the old meeting-house, a simple, one-storeyed building, with the date stone 1697 carved above the doorway. It is hid away up a narrow passage which runs from one of the main streets, and close to it some hundreds of small houses seem waiting for the opening of an Adult School. It is some years now since the meeting was given up ....* [It] *is at present most usefully occupied on week-nights by a men's class in connection with a Church of England Bible-class ....*

Next day was spent by the sources of the Aire, visiting Malham Cove and Gordale Scar, country beloved of Kingsley and Wordsworth. Hard by is .... the little village of Airton with its ancient meeting-house, dating from 1700 [commemorating its purchase, not its inception]. *The old stone building, with the stone bench running round the little paved yard behind it, beside it the quiet grassy graveyard, and the beautiful paddock beyond, seemed all full of good memories. For fifty years this meeting has been one of the smallest in Yorkshire, but most warm is the welcome which visiting Friends receive there. Between sixty and seventy gathered to the meeting for worship at seven o'clock, and at the close we held a meeting for men, mostly young navvies and farm labourers, who listened with interest to a talk on Adult Schools; and finally it was decided to start one in the meeting-house at two o'clock the next Sunday. One of our party had to return home that night, and as we accompanied him on his way towards Hellifield station, six of the younger navvies walked along with us for a mile or two, talking as we went.* A report in the *West Yorkshire Pioneer* for the 22nd of July, 1905, says that the event took place in Airton in the preceding week and that among its leaders were Samuel Davis from York and Henry Cadbury from Birmingham. Other Quaker meetings in the area which these Young Friends found to be still active were at Bentham, Sawley and Settle. Skipton Meeting had ceased some years previously, but Friends retained ownership of Skipton Meeting House and 35 people, not all of whom would have been Quakers, met there for a Wednesday evening meeting for worship organised by the Young Friends.

The Adult School movement began in York in 1848. It was a non-sectarian organisation of Quaker origin fostered by the Rowntree family with the aim of combining teaching in literacy and non-denominational New Testament Bible study with healthy recreation and cultural pursuits. It made strenuous efforts to enhance fellowship and democratic participation, maintaining an elaborate system of monitors and house-to-house visitors. The Yorkshire Adult School Movement began in 1906; from 1911, Airton Summer Schools were managed by the Yorkshire Women's Adult School Union whose purpose was to provide healthful holidays, walks, picnics, excursions, music, games, and illustrated lectures on all manner of subjects for its members. Talks and classes took place in the Meeting House. Among those who lectured for the Summer School were Arthur and Elizabeth Raistrick. In 2004, life-long resident of Airton, Ruth Earnshaw, recollected as a notable treat of her childhood that the Quaker ladies used to come each summer and give concerts which the villagers were invited to attend. Ruth was not a Quaker, but when the Methodist Chapel in Airton closed in 2004, rather than go out of the village to attend church, she joined Friends in our Sunday afternoon meetings for worship in the Airton Meeting House, which she attended regularly for about two years. Writing about Airton in several articles for the *Craven Herald*, in 1912-13, the Rev. W. J. Gomersall said, *Perhaps the most notable feature of Airton life is the mutual service and intercourse which centres round the meeting-house and burial ground. The summer schools are carried on as a branch of the Women's Summer Schools, under the management of the Committee of the Yorkshire Women's Adult School Union – an unsectarian movement originated by the Society of Friends, with the object of giving members a healthful holiday, including walks and talks, excursions and picnics, music and games, and, as a special feature, illustrated lectures on all kinds of subjects.... The Guest House... or Friends' Cottage is presided over during the season by Mrs F. E. Dodson.... There is "The Nook" adjoining the meeting house.... On the roadside stands the "village smithy" under the "spreading tree". The smith's house... is in the centre of the green.* Gomersall published a doggerel verse of his own composition: *Yet still the Quaker house of prayer, And life's last resting ground, Shall breathe the tranquilising air, Which reigns supreme around.... And Airton's Guest House, as of yore, Be still a gate of heaven.* and he quotes a letter sent by F. E. Dodson to the newspaper in 1913 *Our Yorkshire Adult School Union Women's Committee has for two years past used the Guest House as a summer school....* [Gomersall 1914]. Concerning Thomas Braithwaite, who died in 1896 and is buried in Airton, Gomersall says, *quaint "Tommy" Braithwaite, the eccentric stocking knitter, used to give these labours of his hands to poor folk. Poor "Tommy" Braithwaite, I can just remember him.... was always very shy in the presence of ladies.*

Summer School participants stayed in Friends' Cottage across the road from the Meeting House for periods of up to four weeks each year. At other times, it was used, mainly by younger Friends, for simple overnight accommodation. A party of sixth-form students from Ackworth School spent some time there in 1911; the women's Summer School was held there in 1915, and it was used as a holiday guest house in 1918. Although regular Quaker meetings in Airton were discontinued in 1922, about 20 Young Friends including Arnold Waterfall and his brother Sid attended a camp at Scarhouse Farm, Hubberholme in 1930 led by Arthur and *Lill* [Elizabeth] Raistrick. Continuation of the Summer School into the late 1930s is attested by the dates of publication of a set of well-used hymn books that are retained in the Airton Meeting library. Until Ellis House was sold, both it and its adjoining cottage were used to host visiting Friends and the Summer Schools. Thereafter, the cottage, which is now called Ellis Cottage but was then known as Friends' Cottage, was used as a hostel until it too was sold in 1920 for £600. In his unpublished memoirs, Arnold Waterfall says that his father, Joseph, opposed Friends' sale of Ellis Cottage. In retrospect, we may regret these sales. Had the properties been retained in Friends' ownership, the use or letting of Ellis House, Ellis Barn and Ellis Cottage, as they are now called, might have supplied a generous income to support Quaker work. The upper floor of The Barn next to the Meeting House continued to be used as a place where travelling pedlars sometimes displayed their wares in the early decades of the twentieth century. It was also sometimes used by younger Friends as an informal camping place. A photograph taken in 1938 of people gathered outside the Meeting House shows a group of 5 men, 6 women and 9 children, but gives no mention of their names nor of the occasion when it was taken. Since it is a mixed group of various ages, it is perhaps a portrait of those attending a Summer School event or a meeting for worship rather than a group of campers.

Airton was not unaffected by the First World War. For a time, the fabric that covered the framework of early aeroplanes was manufactured at Airton Mill. Arnold Waterfall's grandfather, of whom more below, obtained exemption from conscription in the First World War, as did Arnold in the Second World War. As related in Arnold's memoire, several generations of the Waterfall family had close connections with Airton Meeting. One branch of their family tree has been traced back to a seventeenth-century Quaker, John Waterfall, who lived in the hamlet of Waterfall near Waterhouses in Staffordshire and who had a reputation as a disturber of Established Church services. In 1856, George Waterfall and his wife Anna (Coates) moved from Sutton Forest near York to Holgate Farm in Malhamdale, where they were joined by Arnold's great grandparents, William and Elizabeth (Cartwright). In 1875, William and Elizabeth moved from Holgate Head to Ellis Cottage, in Airton, where Arnold's father, Joseph John Waterfall (1874 – 1943), was brought up by his aunts, his mother having died when he was an infant. Another Waterfall, Arthur, was vice-president of the Malhamdale Temperance Society from 1874 to 1885; at a Band of Hope meeting in 1878 they mustered 44 members under the age of 21 plus 13 adults and eight *non-abstainers*. One of Arnold's grandmothers was Hannah Cartwright: *whilst in her teens she started a Bible class at Airton* that continued until 1866. It seems worthwhile to quote Skipton Meeting's memorial testimony to Arnold's father, Joseph Waterfall. *Born at Holgate Head, Kirkby Malham, on December 24th 1874, he was a member of Airton Meeting in the early years of his life. About 1890, he was employed by the Quaker firm of Hotham & Whiting's, clothing manufacturers of Leeds, and later of Messrs. Myers (late Burnsall) cap manufacturers. During this time, he was an active member of Carleton Hill Meeting, Leeds, becoming leader of the Cycling Group, and lecturer on poetry. In 1910 he came to Skipton taking over the Bookshop from his wife's family. He was still a keen cyclist and great nature lover, having a long association with the Craven Naturalist & Mechanics Institute, and later the Craven Pothole Club. Whilst still at Leeds he had won the Headingly singles title at tennis and was a great help to Sandylands Club. But for his long working hours and refusal to play on Sundays, he would have been of County standard. Later he became scorer to the Tuesday Cricket Club at Skipton. He brought new life into Skipton Meeting, helped the Adult School, and was still in demand for his poetical evenings.*

The early 1940s must have been a busy and exciting time in Airton. From 1943, after a hiatus of approximately twenty years, weekly meetings for worship in the Meeting House were revived and were held throughout the war years, their attendance being augmented by Friends who served as labourers on nearby farms as an alternative to military service, as did Arnold Waterfall, who worked on Kirksdyke Farm. Among those who attended were Phyllis and Arnold Waterfall, the artists Sidney and Constance Pearson who lived in Malham, Mollie Peel and Jennie Bowman from Newfield Hall, John and Pauline Dower of Kirkby Malham, and Elizabeth and Arthur Raistrick, who bicycled over from Linton. Writing in a letter in September 1943, Sidney Pearson mentioned a special Children's Meeting held at Airton one Sunday morning and went on to say, *Our Meeting is now held in the afternoons and we get quite a nice group there* (Diaper 2009, p. 32). No doubt present-day Friends, who also meet for worship at Airton on Sunday afternoons, would say the same. There was also new employment in Airton, though probably not of Quakers, most of whom would have avoided employment in a war-related industry, at the former spinning mill on the River. These buildings now housed a secret factory for the for the production of a vital military supply: the antiseptic Dettol (Reckitt, 1965 p. 108). It is said that the plant's location and function were revealed when an accidental spill caused the River Aire to reek of disinfectabt all the way to Skipton.

In a letter sent to me in 2006, John Stober tells of the start of a new period in the Meeting House's history. *In the early summer of 1941, I was half-way through an engineering course when I wrote to the Friends Relief Service..., asking whether I could help in any way during the university vacation.... I was surprised to be asked to join a work-party at Airton Meeting House and help to prepare for the arrival of evacuated families.*

There was a growing concern for the plight of the population in the bombed cities – the old, families with young children, the handicapped and others – who were being missed by Government evacuation schemes. Friends all over the country were offering emergency accommodation – in some cases little more than meeting house benches for sleeping – and it was soon obvious that this was completely unsuitable for the time that it was likely to be needed. The Relief Service was revived to help with these problems – by improving the facilities available, or by finding, adapting and staffing more suitable premises. Volunteer helpers came from many backgrounds; most were pacifists, but only a minority were Friends.

A work party was set up to do preparatory work and maintenance in hostels in the north of England – at Airton, in the adult school at Settle Meeting House, in the old post office at Bentham, and later in part of the rectory at Bolton-by-Bowland and a large house near Brierfield. Friends also took over the running of a children's home near Clitheroe. We shared our skills, were given tips by friendly tradesmen, and became proficient in a wide range of tasks. The staff at Friends House may have thought that I should be well acquainted with house wiring, but that is not a subject covered by an engineering degree. Fortunately, we were joined temporarily by an ex-electrician, and my knowledge was quickly extended!

At Airton we improved the kitchen [in The Barn] *by putting in a new window and laying a concrete floor, and installed electric wiring throughout the buildings. We lived there, sharing the chores and cooking – and surviving some strange culinary efforts! We spent our off-time exploring the Craven countryside and I have vivid recollections of caving expeditions with Arnold Waterfall of Skipton, who became a good friend....*

We left before the evacuees arrived, but returned from time to time. The months and years passed, and eventually the workparty was operating in hostels from Liverpool and Southport to Filey and from Worcestershire to Edinburgh. We must have laid many thousands of bricks, laid miles of drains, pipes and cables, and painted acres of walls and woodwork – interspersed with digging gardens, building swings and see-saws, making toys – and even cutting hair!!

In 1945 I was seconded to work with French Friends, mainly on transport work, and then had a spell in the Ruhr in Germany before returning to England in October 1946.

It was a very special part of my life, with experiences of all kinds, when I made friendships which have lasted for over sixty years, and it started at Airton – which I always recall with affection as a place of great peace, where I was strangely happy in a war-torn world.

In later years, I came to live in Yorkshire, and was a member of Beverley and Wakefield Meetings. I have peeped in at Airton on a few occasions and I hope that the Meeting House may have many more chapters to add to its long history in this ever-changing world.

Arnold Waterfall was among those who assisted with work on The Barn. When it was completed, he and Phyllis were asked to serve as non-resident wardens. Two evacuee families from Liverpool were housed in the Meeting House: Mrs. Kelbrick had 18-month-old twin boys and an eight-year-old son; Mrs. Baillie had two young sons and a daughter who was born while they lived in Airton. Both families lived in the back part of the Meeting House; one family slept in the gallery, the other behind the screen in the small meeting room. The larger room in the Meeting House continued to be used for Quaker meetings for worship. The two families shared the ground floor of The Barn, which had a low-ceilinged kitchen/living room, a coal bunker and two lavatories. The upper floor of The Barn was by then unsafe. Phyllis did all the cooking in the hostel, not daring to tell the mothers that the *spinach* she served in the spring was in fact nettles. The two mothers and six children remained at Airton for almost a year. During several winters, Airton was isolated by heavy snowfalls; the worst, in 1941, lasted for seven weeks.

In March 1943 the Settle Adult School was adapted to house elderly evacuees. After two unsuccessful appointments of Wardens for this scheme, the Waterfalls took over for a few months until that scheme was closed. When, early the next year, tenancy of the cottage adjacent to the Airton Meeting House, The Nook, became vacant Arnold and Phyllis moved in and became Resident Wardens paying three shillings per week as rent, of which six pence was reimbursed as payment for their caretaking of the Meeting House and The Barn. They served as Wardens until 1969. Largely at their own expense, they enlarged The Nook by incorporating into it the northern end of the upstairs of The Barn, restructured as two additional bedrooms, and by installing a first-floor bathroom. When this building was refurbished in 2011, the cottage was restored to its original size; what had been additional bedrooms for The Nook became the present bunk- and shower-rooms in The Barn.

As temporary residents, including some Quakers, moved away from Malhamdale at the end of the war, attendance at Airton Meeting decreased. An Allowed Meeting [a no-longer used status for Quaker Meetings that were too small to conduct their own administrative affairs] had been started in Linton in 1945. Although this lasted for less than two years, it diverted some of what was already a declining attendance from Airton Meeting, which ceased in 1948. Airton was not the only local Friends meeting to be poorly attended in the post-war period. By 1951 Settle Meeting had lapsed, as it had only three potentially active members: Winifred and Eddie Horner and Bernard Holmes. The Waterfalls were asked to assist with its revival, which they did in preference to keeping an active meeting for worship at Airton. At times the Waterfall parents and children were the only worshippers in Settle Meeting House on a Sunday morning. By 1957, Settle Meeting had increased to an average attendance of about eight. In 1963, acting as Clerk of the relevant Trust Funds Committee, which held funds from the several Ellis bequests, from other bequests and from the sale of several disused Quaker meeting houses, the Waterfalls arranged for part of the old Settle Adult School to be converted to serve as a cottage for Resident Wardens. Ruth and Kevin Petrie were appointed to this position in 1964. It was later occupied by their daughter, Alison Tyas.

Young Friends' use of The Barn was much increased after the Second World War, with the Waterfalls' active encouragement. When camping in The Barn, Young Friends also used the Meeting House for occasional meetings for worship; I have been told that they sometimes referred to its hard wooden benches as *bum numbers*. In his memoirs, Roger Waterfall says that, *When we arrived, the place hadn't been used for years except as the occasional kipping down place for Young Friends. The* [first] *floor was full of holes and really unsafe, and the roof leaked in several places. After the evacuees had left, Young Friends took over the stable, to run it as a Youth Hostel and we became their treasurers and wardens.* They persuaded the Trustees who owned the building to have it re-roofed and themselves managed to raise sufficient funds to put in a new staircase and beech-wood floor. That was in 1950. Part of the cost was met by holding *6d hops* on Saturday nights, with dancing to records played on the Waterfalls' gramophone: Progressive Barn Dance, Moonlight Saunter, Dashing White Sergeant, Square Tango, and The Lancers plus a few more modern waltzes and foxtrots. After the dances, the Young Friends who were staying overnight slept on the new first floor with a movable screen separating the men and women.

A Young Friend, Peter Leadbeater (1937 – 1957), who attended Leeds Modern Grammar School, was most active in organising Yorkshire Young Friends' weekends and holidays, for which he kept logs detailing the dates, who was present, their activities and, most importantly, what they had to eat; his brother, Michael, has kindly lent these to me. *Spud peeling and wood gathering filled the morning with rainy intervals.... appetites satisfied, we began the exacting job of lighting the bonfire.... Returning at 9:30 (moonlit evening) to dance down supper, we forgot fatigue and blisters. Such was our enthusiasm that this continued until 12:45 when tea was served again.... Never was so much breakfast consumed by so few in such a short time.... Rain!! table tennis & dancing & frequent brews of tea.... Sunday – after meeting, the party set off in a westerly direction, towards Settle, dinner being consumed at Scalber Falls....* Peter's logs and sketched drawings pertain to eighteen weekend and longer events over a period of five years, starting in November 1951. There were also two weekends for members of the Christian Union which Peter founded at his school. While some of the work parties involved fewer than ten, most of the holidays were larger with the participation of as many as 25 young men and women. Each year there was a, usually wet, bonfire and fireworks – some homemade – in November and a *Christmas party* in January. Some Young Friends bicycled from Leeds to Airton, setting a record time of less than two hours, though about four hours riding in rain and against a headwind is more frequently mentioned. Others came by bus or train to Bell Busk or walked from Coniston Cold; only a few came on motorbikes or were brought by car. Their activities were largely self-supervised, although Phyllis and Arnold Waterfall seem always to have been around to lend a hand when it was wanted and on several occasions to lead potholing and caving expeditions. There were also work-parties to mend furniture, scrub and repaint the inside of The Barn and once, in 1954, to creosote the floor of the Meeting House and its gallery. It was the efforts of one such party that applied shiny, lead-based grey paint to all the benches and woodwork in the Meeting House. Incomplete removal of that paint has resulted in the ancient oak's present blotchy appearance. Always there were long walks and dancing to the Waterfalls' gramophone; when numbers were uneven, some used chairs as partners. There was much brewing of tea, peeling of potatoes, and meetings for worship in the *frigid M*eeting House. Many Yorkshire Friends now look back with great pleasure on those events of more than sixty years ago.

Jill Sykes and Nora Stanhope were two of these Young Friends. In November, 2018 they reminisced with one another, and Jill sent me the following in an e-mail. *My hostel holidays would cover the 3 years of late 1951 through 1954. Nora would probably go two years before and one year after me. Nora talked of country-dancing the nights away till 3:00 in the morning. Dennis Binns always took a gramophone and records for our repertoire of country/old-time dances. No wonder that the neighbours complained one time, and to say sorry, we spent the next two days rehearsing then performing a show for them in the Methodist church hall. Our visits were usually at half-terms so only 2 or 3 days, but usually included 2 long walks. Padded sleeping bags hadn't been invented. Nora remembers mattresses on the floor. I remember a very hard surface of new floorboards, no doubt with lots of blankets. After dancing we put up some light-weight partitions across the upper room and slept boys one side, girls the other. I remember the boys sleeping in the meeting house gallery one year when there were lots of us. One winter weekend I cooked a Christmas dinner for 11 of us on two primus stoves. I know the turkey came out of a tin. The Waterfalls, Phyllis and Arnold were always kind and helpful. Their two children would be school age then. My photos show a work-party at rest one February, which included Peter Leadbeater, who fell off a mountain in 1959* [sic]. *The groups were mainly Leeds Young Friends, but my photos show what must have been an all-Yorkshire gathering too.*

In order to help with managing The Barn, Phyllis Waterfall typed out a set of *General Rules:* .... *The Meeting House must be always clean and tidy, and the premises quiet when being used for Meeting for Worship.... The whole premises to be left clean (including ashes and flues of fires) and clear of all food and liquids etc. Leave the place as you would like to find it... Expect visitors any time. This being one of the oldest Meeting Houses in the Dales and of much interest historically....* The Waterfalls also circulated a more formal advertisement for The Barn. *The Yorkshire Q.M. Trust Property consists of the Meeting House... and the old Barn (known locally as "Klondyke"), now the Hostel. It consists of two good bedrooms (or one very large with h. and c.), entrance hall with two lavs, and kitchen cum dining room.... canvas beds with blankets.... As the Hostel is often booked up by organisations for a month at a time, early booking is essential. Comfortable accommodation for seven of each sex – or a few more if the gallery in the Meeting house is used for extra bedroom. A delightful retreat for Families or Week-end Study Groups.*

Intermittent use of The Barn by Young Friends continued for several decades. In an e-mail sent to me in January 2019, John Gilham wrote that, *During the 1990s I helped lead a group of teenagers from York Friargate's* [Friargate Friends Meeting] *Link Group on a mountain biking weekend, once a year for about 10 years, staying each year at the Airton hostel* [The Barn]. *There were usually 14 of us, usually 4 adults (3 men, one woman) and 10 children (at least 2 girls always included). We took the bicycles in a hired van to Skipton station on Friday evening while the rest of the party took the train from York to Skipton. We then cycled from Skipton to Airton where the van party had gone ahead and prepared an evening meal. Saturday and Sunday were spent getting muddy and wet and excited on trails round to Malham, Scalber Force and Otterburn. There was the queue down the upstairs corridor for the shower. Memorable features were huge breakfasts for 14 prepared on the hostel's cooker with its minimal supply of pans, and evening bicycle games on the meadows by the river followed by long noisy games of UNO. On Sunday afternoon we tidied up and repeated the process of getting back to Skipton station. We always held a Meeting for Worship in the Meeting House before we left.*

Arnold and Phyllis served as Resident Wardens at Airton for twenty-five years, and he as Clerk of the Trust Funds Committee that managed Quaker properties and charities in the compass of Brighouse, Leeds and Settle Area Meetings from 1956 to 1965. During this time, Arnold followed his father in continuing to run the Skipton Bookshop and in a variety of energetic outdoor pursuits. Regrettably, in 1965 earlier verbal arrangements were forgotten and disagreement arose over an attempt to increase the rent charged to the Waterfalls for their tenancy of The Nook. The outcome was that they moved away. For the remainder of the twentieth century, The Barn continued to be used as a hostel, but after the Waterfalls left it was less actively managed and there was less maintenance of the Meeting House. Concerning the burial ground at Airton, Arnold Waterfall says in his memoir, *during our time at Airton, four of our family died and their ashes were buried at Airton. One day we received a registered parcel and whilst I was signing the chit, I mentioned to the postman that they were Auntie Lillie's ashes. He was so shocked he nearly dropped the parcel....* The Cartwrights and the Waterfalls account for most of the stones in the burial ground. The Cartwrights were relatives of the Waterfall family and also of Brontë Bedford-Payne, a more recent member of Airton Meeting. Several memorial stones have been added since Arnold's time and the burial ground remains open, but only for the interment of Friends who are closely connected with Airton Meeting.

An undated mid-twentieth-century record of the trusts and funds managed by the Brighouse, Leeds and Settle Joint Trust Funds shows that the Airton Meeting House, Hostel and Cottage generated an annual income of £14 6s 0d from rent plus £7 17s 4d from investments, while the Alice Ellis Trust Fund for the poor and needy had a capital of £1,041, and the William and Alice Ellis Apprentices Fund had a capital of £545. These were subsequently amalgamated into the holdings of a Joint Trust Fund and no longer used for their original purposes. A financial review in 1982 showed a net income of just £21 from all of the Airton Trust Property. That year saw the appointment of a new management committee. Alteration of The Barn in 1983 provided three small bunkrooms and a shower on the first floor, with an improved kitchen downstairs. Use of the facilities increased immediately. From an average gross income from overnight accommodation of £920 in 1983 it rose to £4,881 in 1995, but then decreased towards the end of the century as its managing committee became less active and The Barn increasingly in need of repair and modernisation. Before the resumption of Quaker meetings for worship in 2000, little attempt was made to maintain an active Quaker presence in Malhamdale except that once or twice a year from about 1970 widely advertised meetings for worship were attended by many Yorkshire and Lancashire Friends. In 1997, members of the existing management committee for the Airton Trust Property asked to be relieved of their duties and there were suggestions that the property be sold. After much discussion, with some Friends saying that they considered the property to be unviable, a new management committee appointed by Settle Monthly Meeting was tasked with finding some more profitable use for The Barn. At that point, the antiquity and historical significance of the Meeting House were not known and the possibility of resuming Quaker worship in it was not considered. The new committee took an energetic approach towards restoration of the Meeting House and Barn and promotion of their use by a wide variety of community groups and events, and a major fundraising campaign was instituted to support this ambition. Occasional use of the Meeting House for worship was resumed in 2000, with regular use twice a month starting in 2002.

Following the Waterfalls, Maurice and Margaret Blades served as Resident Wardens from 1968, and George and Josie Parker from Easter 1986 to October 2010. After repairs and refurbishment of The Nook, Ursel Boyer became Resident Friend at the start of 2011, Floe Shakespeare in 2012 and Simon Watkins in 2015. Since 2012, use of The Barn and the Meeting House by community groups and others has increased greatly. In the first eight months of 2014, it was estimated that about 200 people stayed overnight, and 1,200 used The Barn for daytime and evening classes, concerts, meetings and events. In addition, about 6,800 members of walking groups, touring parties and casual visitors paid briefer visits to view the historic meeting house; it also served as a polling station.

Interview with Phyllis Waterfall: on the 20th of January 1998, Richard Harland had a conversation with Phyllis Waterfall of Skipton Preparative [now Local] Meeting, in the course of which she told him the following, which he recorded as a continuous narrative, as if in direct speech. *Before World War Two, I lived with Arnold over Waterfall's bookshop, in which he worked, in Sheep Street, Skipton, but I knew Airton well. As a child, I used to come with my parents to the Adult School summer schools, when we were accommodated in the house opposite, which was owned by Friends. Later, as a Young Friend, I stayed with YFs from Leeds in the hostel. Only the ground floor was used; it had kitchen, dormitory and toilets. We never used upstairs because the floor was unsafe.*

When war came, there was a Quaker committee who arranged accommodation for evacuees in Friends' properties. I think both London and Yorkshire Friends were in this, including a Rowntree. I assume it was by arrangement with Liverpool Friends that two families were chosen for Airton: two mothers and altogether five pre-school children. ....

Arnold's commitment to pacifism was largely due to Arthur Raistrick whom he much admired.

Arnold felt he would be more useful farming than in the [book] *shop. Some customers were staying away from the shop because of pacifism there, so he took a job farming at Airton. There was no hostility to him in the village. We were appointed to look after the evacuees at the Meeting House. The caretaker's cottage* [the Nook] *was occupied by a tenant. Edward Sea. A Leeds Friend, had a holiday cottage in the row opposite and he generously allowed us to live there.*

The evacuees slept in the back part of the Meeting House, one family in the gallery and the other behind the screen below. The main meeting room was boarded off, so you came in through the door into a [temporary] *passage and turned right to the bedrooms and left to the meeting room. The families used the downstairs of the hostel for kitchen and living room. I made meals for the families and the mothers helped. There were shops in Airton: Taylor's and the post office, and a butcher's van came from Long Preston and a grocery van once a week.*

It took the families a long time to get used to life in Airton, even not to be frightened of cows. When told that milk comes from cows, one of the children said, "No, ours comes from bottles". Arnold would take the children up to the farm sometimes. The villagers were friendly to them. The two fathers visited every two or four weeks, probably alternating....

After the war, the families went home. Arnold and I liked Airton and we wanted to stay. The caretaker's cottage became vacant, so we lived there for very many years. Regular meetings for worship were started. Jean(?) Dower would come from Kirkby Malham and Arthur and Elizabeth Raistrick would cycle from Linton. Also we helped to re-start Settle Meeting, which had been closed for many years – we would cycle over. Incidentally, I also started the Airton Women's Institute; till then we had to go to Kirkby Malham W.I.

11. Into the twenty-first century

Not long after I moved to Threshfield in 1997, Settle Monthly Meeting asked me to serve as Convenor of the Management Committee that was responsible for the Airton Trust Property, and as a Trustee of the Brighouse, Leeds and Settle Monthly Meetings' Joint Buildings Charity which owned it. The property was then in a poor state of repair, with a partially unroofed Meeting House and a damp and decaying stone barn that was fitted out as a self-catering bunkhouse, but no longer attracted much use. The appointment seemed to be an instance of giving the newcomer a job that no one else wanted to do; several Friends said as much. Friends were then unaware that my previous experience as an archaeologist and in several other capacities made this a very suitable appointment. This was the start of more than a decade of discussions, work and fundraising that culminated in the reopening of a restored Meeting House and cottage together with a comprehensively refurbished Barn, repaired garden wall, newly paved access paths and repaved area in front of the Meeting House. The small garden store room was also repaired and reroofed and part of the lawn in front of The Barn sculpted to provide an almost-flat seating area.

In 1998, six or eight Friends began meeting from time to time at the home of Elma and Richard Harland in Grassington. Among much else, we discussed the possibility of holding regular Quaker meetings for worship in Grassington and when Richard spoke of his long-cherished desire to see meetings for worship resumed in the old Airton Meeting House, we agreed to attempt this. Starting in 2000, Quaker meetings for worship were held twice a month in the unheated and partly unroofed Airton Meeting House, but only in the summer. Two years later, it was decided to meet all year around. For the following two winters until the Meeting House roof was finally repaired, a valiant few brought blankets and huddled around a foul-smelling paraffin gas heater, with puddles of rainwater at our feet. From that small beginning, in 2004 Settle Monthly Meeting accepted Airton as a *recognised* (a now-obsolete designation for Quaker meetings that were deemed too small or transient to take on administrative responsibilities) meeting. Then for a few months, we met in the recently-closed Methodist chapel in Airton, until our Meeting House was fully repaired and reopened in 2008. The Nook, which is the Resident Friend's Cottage, was restored in 2010.

The Barn was also in a very poor state of repair. A fire-safety officer who inspected the building at my request said that if we did not close it voluntarily, he would issue a compulsory order for us to do so. It was closed for about eight months in 2004 while essential work was done to improve its sanitation and fire-safety. Among other faults, there was no fire-door at the top of a steep wooden staircase leading to the first-floor bunkrooms, an electric clothes-drying cabinet with frayed wiring was located under these stairs, there were neither fire alarm nor emergency lighting, and the bunkrooms were overcrowded. A kitchen/social room on the ground floor was ill-ventilated, cramped and uninviting, with perpetually damp walls, rotten cupboards with collapsing shelves, and a ceiling height of little more than seven feet. The main entrance to The Barn was then the smaller and upper of the two entrances that now open onto the Meeting House grounds. From it, one went down a few steps into a small lobby whose sloping concrete floor witnessed the building's previous functions as a stable or barn, or up a narrow flight of open-tread stairs on the right. The area which now comprises the library and the main entrance to The Barn had been a garage accessed from the Green in front of Airton House, but was by this time a junk-filled storeroom used by tenants of The Nook. For a few years, after minimal essential repairs were made and a party of Quaker Voluntary Action volunteers cleaned and redecorated the walls, we attempted to continue The Barn's function as a three-bedroom hostel offering very basic overnight accommodation. When this proved to be financially unviable, it was decided to lower the ground floor, remove all interior walls, partitions and stairs and to restructure it internally as a multi-function community centre with a single bunkroom. During the course of this work, it was found that two ancient, massive beams that were intended to support the first floor had so rotted at their ends that instead of the staircase depending on the floor for its support, the staircase was the only support for the upstairs floor at its southern end. These beams, which must originally have been roof timbers, were too rotten to be retained. Portions of one of them were made into a pair of turned wooden bowls which Airton Meeting now uses for charitable collections. The Barn was reopened in 2011. Subsequently, further work has been done on the roofs of the Meeting House, The Nook and The Barn. About the time The Barn was re-opened, a new long-distance, coast-to-coast cycleway, The Way of the Roses, was initiated, and fortuitously for us Airton is located close to the midpoint of this route. Thanks to well-directed marketing efforts by our Voluntary Resident Friends, The Barn has become known as a convenient overnight stopping point for cyclists; it has also taken on some of the community functions, including hosting civil parish meetings and serving as a polling station, that had been performed by Airton Methodist Hall, which closed in 2004. Income generated by these varied uses of the premises largely pays for their upkeep and maintenance.

In keeping with Friend's principles, we did not apply for lottery-funded grants to assist with any of this work, but instead relied on donations from several hundreds of individuals and from many Quaker meetings, plus grants from 54 different charities and funding bodies. Approximately £300,000 was raised and spent on repairing the Meeting House, The Barn and the garden walls and shed. The Buildings Charity, which owned the property, contributed £50,000 of this total. In addition, they financed the restoration of The Nook including essential repairs to its roof, which were delayed until 2016. On average, each grant application took about ten hours to complete. Several unsuccessful grant applications and tentative enquiries were made for each that was successful and appeal letters and leaflets were sent to every Local and Area Meeting in England. Added to this were very many hours spent with architects and builders and with a not always supportive Committee appointed by Settle Monthly Meeting. One way and another, it all added up to a very large number of hours devoted to restoring the property. For several years, convening the Airton Trust Property Management Committee was almost a fulltime occupation. Although managed by Airton Local Meeting on behalf of Craven and Keighley Area Meeting, the Airton Trust Property continued to be owned by the Buildings Charity until 2018. In that year, the charity was disbanded, its assets dispersed and ownership of the Airton Trust Property transferred to Craven and Keighley Area Meeting. Bringing the story up to date, in January 2020, Airton Local Meeting includes five members of the Religious Society of Friends (Quakers) plus a fluctuating number of more-or-less frequent attenders at our meetings for worship, which are held on two Sunday afternoons a month throughout the year. Meetings for church affairs [business meetings] are held approximately once every two months. Usually, about ten people comprise our regular meetings for worship, including members, frequent attenders and casual visitors. Among those who belong to or support Airton Meeting, only our Voluntary Resident Friend lives in Malhamdale. Two Friends live in Selside, one in Cracoe and one in Threshfield; our most supportive attenders live in Hebden and in Steeton.

The Airton Appeal. Repair and restoration of the Meeting House and grounds in 2007 and 2008, including partial rebuilding of the garden perimeter walls, cost £105,000. This was paid for by grants from charitable trusts and funds and by many donations from individuals and from Quaker meetings in England. Essential repairs to The Nook, completed in 2010 at a cost £31,000, were paid for by the Brighouse, Leeds and Settle Monthly Meetings' Joint Buildings Charity. Repairs and extensive refurbishment of The Barn, substantially completed in 2011 at a cost of somewhat over £190,000, were paid for by individual donations, grants from charitable trusts and funds, and by direct fundraising, with a contribution from the Buildings Charity. Principal contributors to the Airton Appeal, which ran from 2006 to 2010, were the following.

Donations of £5,000 and higher: Allchurches; Brighouse, Leeds and Settle Monthly Meetings' Joint Buildings Charity; Britain Yearly Meeting, Meeting Houses Funds; Edward Cadbury Trust; Craven District Council; Garfield Weston Foundation; National Churches Trust; Quakers in Yorkshire Forrest Fund; Sir James Reckitt Charity; Yorkshire Dales Millennium Trust Sustainable Development Fund; Yorventure; two private donations.

Donations between £1,000 and £5,000: Craven Trust; E.M. Ellis Trust; Historic Churches Yorkshire Trust; Leche Trust; Manifold Trust; North Yorkshire County Council Craven Area Committee; Skipton Local Meeting; W.F. Southall Trust; C.B. and H.H. Taylor 1984 Trust; Wensleydale and Swaledale Monthly Meeting Trust; Westcroft Trust; two private donations.

Additional Donations came from: Bryan Lancaster's Trust; C. and E. Morelands' Trust; W. A. Cadbury Trust; R. E. Chadwick Trust; Mollie Croysdale Trust; Hawkes Charity; K. Higginbottom Trust; Morland's Charitable Trust; O. Moreland Trust; Oakdale Trust; P.M. Lovell Trust; Albert Reckett Trust; P. and D. Shepherd Trust; very many Quaker local meetings; several hundred individual donations; and a variety of concerts and other direct fundraising activities.

While many Friends actively supported and contributed to the restoration of the Airton Trust Property and revival of a Quaker meeting for worship at Airton, six individuals were constantly involved over a period of fifteen or more years. Three of us, Hilary Fenten, Wilf Fenten, and I continue to be active members of Airton Local Meeting. Three others are no longer with us: Richard Harland, Kevin Berry, and Brontë Bedford-Payne. Each of them deserves to be remembered in connection with the Airton Meeting House.

Richard Harland *Without a knowledge of Quaker History our corporate life is diminished .... To understand our history is to understand ourselves.* These quotations, which are paraphrased from an essay by John Punshon (2004, p. 80), epitomise Richard's enthusiasm for ferreting out the details of Quaker history especially in its local aspects, in Malhamdale, in Skipton and in the Craven area. This interest, which was fostered by his close friendship with Arthur Raistrick, he generously shared. Richard produced several carefully researched and elegantly worded ephemeral pamphlets and leaflets to celebrate anniversaries in the history of Skipton Friends Meeting and to welcome visitors to our historic meeting houses. Together, he and I produced a now superseded booklet on the history of *Airton Meeting House and some of the Friends who Worshipped There* that was widely distributed in support of the fundraising appeal for the restoration of the Meeting House. For that booklet and for part of this present work, Richard trawled with meticulous thoroughness through Quaker archives and minute books at Friends House, London, in the Brotherton Library at Leeds University, and wherever else he could find them, producing detailed lists of persons, dates and places of undoubted accuracy, but usually lacking source references. My part has been to supplement these with material from published works and to attempt to build from the minutiae a coherent narrative, based on facts where they existed and on most probable conjectures where such were needed. While doing this research, it became clear that for a few significant decades in the seventeenth century, people and events in the Craven area generally and especially in Airton and Skipton played a central role in the formation of the social and theological movement that grew into the Religious Society of Friends.

From time to time Richard and I talked about producing a comprehensive work on the history of Quakerism in Malhamdale, but somehow the more pressing demands of restoring the ancient Meeting House and sustaining a revived Quaker meeting for worship always took precedence and the book was never begun. Eventually I inherited some of his files of miscellaneous papers, mostly in a tight and almost illegible script, a few headed *from the files of Arthur Raistrick*, and several unfinished drafts of two proto-chapters, which have been consolidated and are included here as chapter seven. A short piece, *Welcome Friends*, was originally written by Richard as a handout for visitors to Farfield Meeting House, near Addingham, who knew little about Quakerism. Rewritten in 2008 for visitors to Airton Meeting House, it is a good example of the quality of his writing and of his Quakerism.

In these rooms, Quaker meetings for worship have been held for more than 350 years. Our meetings are based on silent, expectant waiting as we try to come nearer to each other and to God.

We have found that to gather in silence as a group can be calming, healing, creative, challenging and energising, and that this experience is available to all who seek it.

While you are here, you may like to sit quietly, perhaps for a few minutes, perhaps for longer. Just sit and listen to sounds outside and within the room, to your own breathing, to the promptings of love and kindness in your heart. Then think of goodness in the hearts of each of the others in your group. That will be enough.

Kevin Berry Another Friend who was most closely associated with the restoration of the Meeting House and resumption of regular meetings for worship at Airton was Kevin Berry. I first met him about a year after a few of us had begun holding Quaker meetings for worship in the unregenerate and partly unroofed Meeting House. Initially, he did not come to these, but when we opened the Meeting House to the public for a Historic Buildings Open Day he came to view in the morning and said he would return in the afternoon to take a turn at greeting visitors. No matter that he did not return that day; soon thereafter he became closely involved with the life of the new meeting and with the tremendous amount of work involved in the Airton Trust Property's restoration.

For a time, the Committee tasked with managing and restoring the property was burdened with several members of very diverse opinions: some wanted to sell all or part of the property for housing development, some wanted it to be left quietly to decay, some wanted it improved but did not themselves want to work towards the improvement. Initially, only a stubborn minority wanted improvements and was willing to work towards their realisation. A particular difficulty was in finding a Treasurer who would attend meetings, answer e-mails and make reports. After sitting quietly through one or two rather frustrating committee meetings, Kevin volunteered that he would like to be one of the few Friends who would comprise a sub-committee to be actively involved in fundraising and that he would like to be its Treasurer. When questioned as to whether he realised what he would be taking on, he replied that he would like to do it, he would enjoy it. Even while doubting the enjoyment, his offer was accepted with gratitude and relief. Thereafter, work progressed more easily as he became increasingly involved in all aspects of the restoration of the Airton Meeting House, refurbishment of The Barn, and participation in our meetings for worship.

Fundraising, appointment of an architect, design consultation, morale boosting, work parties; it was a long haul and Kevin stuck with it for more than a decade. Whenever there was a task that no one else would undertake, he would sit quietly for a while and then volunteer that he would like to do it, he really would. Some of these, like coping with the not entirely satisfactory appointment of a new Resident Friend at Airton, were very burdensome. Others were lighter. When we were encumbered with half-a-dozen surplus fire extinguishers, he offered to buy several because *they might be useful* around his home. When the Airton Friends Meeting needed a Clerk, that service, too, was just what Kevin would like to perform. On many of the seemingly small, but actually quite important decisions about the redesign of The Barn and its furnishings, Kevin and I, supported all the way by his wife Pat and by my husband David, were left to do whatever we thought best. Kevin remained faithful to the task of seeing the work through to completion. Without his calm, steady presence, restoration of the Airton Trust Property might not have been accomplished.

Brontë Bedford-Payne The following paragraphs are an appreciation of the life of Brontë Bedford-Payne prepared by Airton Local Meeting, accepted as a testimony by Craven and Keighley Area Meeting, by Quakers in Yorkshire, and by Britain Yearly Meeting in 2018. *In her teenage years, Brontë and her sister, Elizabeth, lived with their aunt's family, who kept sheep at Drebley near Bolton Abbey. She explored widely on her bicycle, coming to know and to love the uplands of the Yorkshire Dales, its people, birds, flowers, buildings, history and the lay and feel of the land. On one such tour, she first visited Airton Meeting House, where a relative of hers had formerly been a resident warden, and in the restoration of which she was later to be closely interested. The habits of keeping a personal diary and of making notes of what she observed served her well in later life, when she produced several books and gave talks on local history and related topics. She was an excellent public speaker.*

During the war years, Leeds Grammar School for Girls was evacuated to Bolton Abbey. Brontë attended as a day pupil and went on to study dentistry at University College in London, an unusual career for a woman in those days. She married a fellow dentist, Richard Arthur Bedford-Payne, on 13 September, 1952, at Bolton Abbey. They raised two children and had a thriving practice in Letchworth Garden City. Brontë had several placements as a schools' dental surgeon, including six months as a locum in Orkney in the early 1970s.

Eventually, the call of the north became irresistible and in 1975 they bought Low Mill, on the Grassington side of Linton Falls, where they established themselves as the local dentists with a side-line in fish farming. Brontë specialised in children's dentistry. She had a wonderful ability to relate to people, so much so that decades after she had retired people would say with pleasure, "she used to be my dentist when I was a child". During this time, they had memorable caravan holidays with their family and friends. Brontë also had a rich creative life, as a pianist, a writer, and an outstanding needle worker. While living in Letchworth and at Low Mill, she and Richard were active Attenders of Quaker Meetings. They each joined Skipton Meeting (Settle Monthly Meeting) in 1994, a few months before Richard died. A year later, Brontë moved to Summers Barn in Grassington. In 2012 she transferred the listing of her membership to Airton Local Meeting (Craven and Keighley Area Meeting).

Brontë was active in the Grassington Peace Group and in the Upper Wharfedale Field Society, which she served as General Secretary for ten years, and then as its President in 1999. In 2001, she was made an Honorary Life Member of the Field Society, for which she organised study groups, projects and field visits. In the last days of her final illness, she was concerned that a trip which had been arranged months previously and which she had intended to lead should go ahead as planned so that its participants would not be disappointed.

Among all her varied interests, Brontë also gave much time to Friends. She served as an Elder of Skipton Local Meeting and as an editor of the Meeting's newsletter; she was a

Trustee and frequent Resident Friend at Glenthorne, the Quaker guest house in Grasmere. She was one of the first Friends to be interested in and actively support restoration of the Airton Meeting House, joining with a few others to huddle in blankets in a circle around a noxious paraffin heater as we worshipped in the partly-unroofed building for almost two years before it was repaired. On one such occasion, she went out to hush a noisy party of walkers who were peering into the windows of what they thought was a derelict building and was just in time to hear one of them say to the others, "Look! They're in there. They're doing it. They're doing it right now!". She explained that "it" was Quaker worship, not witchcraft and sent them on their way.

In 2000, Brontë was inspired by an article in The Friend to create an Airton tapestry panel. Typical of her ability to bring people together, the nine whom she assembled for this project included embroiderers and non-needle workers, local school children, members of Skipton Meeting, and residents of Malhamdale. Brontë wrote of the project, "We were not an established group of men and women looking for something to do .... we were a group of local people, not all Quakers, who came together, purely to create an embroidered panel, a thing well made, which would add to the rich heritage of historical interest in Malhamdale".

Several Friends have said that what they have valued most about knowing Brontë was the pleasure of her company. Travelling with her on country roads to visit farming friends or a favourite wildflower meadow and simple trips between Grassington and Airton were enlivened by her pointing out the origins of scars on the landscape, places where her relatives had lived, the ages and purposes of particular walls and buildings, an ancient rabbit warren or an archaeological site. She was thoroughly embedded in the Yorkshire Dales and generous in sharing her love and knowledge of it. Visitors to her home were warmly received, with tea and much-appreciated home-made ginger biscuits. She was equally welcoming to newcomers to Skipton and to Airton Local Meetings. One Friend said, "I will always remember how welcoming, reassuring and informative she was towards me as a newcomer". Other Friends have said, "she was always approachable and easy to talk to .... sometimes a bit timid, but at the same time there was real steel in there.... there was a touch of gentility.... Brontë's capacity for recognising the abilities of others.... working with Brontë was a privilege as well as a delight".

Brontë was never a very conspicuous Quaker. She shuddered at the idea of wearing a lapel badge that said, "I am a Quaker ask me why", but she kept our testimonies and she lived her Quakerism to the full. In doing so, she enriched the lives of all who knew her.

12.   The Buildings and their Furnishings

Having set the scene in previous chapters, we can now recapitulate and look more closely at the early-seventeenth-century Dissenters' meeting place which over the intervening centuries has been minimally adapted to become the Airton Meeting House that stands today. Evidence of the building's age and architectural history is detailed in the book, *Hidden in Plain Sight, history and architecture of the Airton Meeting House* (Phillipson and Armstrong 2017) and is not repeated here. That this building stands on and reflects the footprint of an even older stone barn is indicated by its massive foundation stones and by reused cruck beams in its roof. Unlike the present Meeting House, precursor barn would have faced onto the street. What looks like the threshold of its subsidiary door or mucking-out hole can be seen in the configuration of foundation stones on the east gable end of the Meeting House. We can envisage the building which preceded our meeting house as a stone barn very similar proportions, but somewhat larger than, High Laithe, which is preserved on the edge of Grimwith Reservoir. The Meeting House which Gervase Benson described in his memoirs as *a barn in a field in Airton* was probably about 50 years old when he preached there in 1657 or 1658; it stood on its own in a field and it was barn-like in appearance, though not in its function. Responding to the 1686 Act of Indulgence, Farfield Meeting House, near Addingham, was built in 1689. It is of similar style and proportions to the Airton Meeting House and thus gives a good impression of how the Airton Meeting House must have looked before its roof was raised. Both were erected by workmen well versed in the local style of barn construction at the behest of people who had no desire for architectural refinement or elaboration. Both were purpose-built for religious worship; neither has had any history of use as an agricultural building. The first recorded interment in the Quaker burial ground alongside the Airton Meeting House was of Isabell Wilkinson in 1663, although the oldest grave marker dates only to 1859, as earlier Friends did not choose to commemorate individuals in that way.

The Resident Friend's cottage, The Nook, is at least partly superimposed on the same ancient foundation plinth as the Meeting House, replacing an earlier small outbuilding at the west end of the precursor barn. Some features of the fireplace in The Nook and a possible door recess in the living room wall to the left of the fireplace suggest that this wall may be a surviving remnant of precursor barn.

Extensive renovations in 2010 temporarily exposed the original south face of the early-seventeenth-century cottage. This wall now functions as the ground-floor party wall between The Nook and the library of The Barn. The blocked remains of a window and an external doorway were revealed in the cottage's south-facing wall. Their unusual position aligned them with the entrance to the Meeting House, and suggests an approximately similar age for both structures. This inference is supported by the style of The Nook's chimney stack, which is older than the one on the east gable of the Meeting House; the latter dates to work that Alice Ellis had done in 1710. The south-facing window and doorway of the cottage were both rendered inaccessible when, also in 1710, a staircase was put into the living room of The Nook in order to access its newly-constructed first floor.

Configuration of the quoins on the Meeting House's northern face between it and The Nook indicates that construction of the cottage's ground-floor postdates that of the Meeting House, perhaps only by a few months or years. Other architectural evidence confirms historical records that its construction predates its enlargement in 1710. The cottage's general layout and some features, including the early seventeenth-century, or possibly older, chimney which serves the probably eighteenth-century fireplace in its living room, indicate that it was built as a residence. Records to the effect that in 1710 Alice Ellis had a cottage built on the site of a former stable, at the same time as the building we call The Barn was erected, must refer to rebuilding and enlargement by the addition of an upper storey to the existing small cottage, rather than its total demolition and replacement. Ambiguously, the 1700 purchase deed for the property refers to a *house, barn or stable*. We may thus think of The Nook as having grown out of successive remodellings of what may have begun as a simple shelter attached to the original barn on whose foundation the Meeting House was constructed. Later, it became housing, probably for a resident Friend. This was done in some early Quaker meeting places in order to prevent their seizure and destruction as illicit places of worship. Since the Meeting House and The Nook roofs are closely, but not perfectly aligned, it appears that the Meeting House roof was raised in 1710, at the same time as the small cottage, which by that date may have been used as a stable, was enlarged and the building we now call The Barn was constructed as a new free-standing stable with a hayloft over. At that time the staircase and upper floor were added to the cottage, creating the unusual layout of an under-stairs passage between its pantry and living room, obscuring the original external door and window, and requiring their replacement by new ones inserted in the north wall facing onto the road. The Nook porch is a later, probably nineteenth-century, addition. The former coal house, now a washroom, abutting the porch is later still.

A very long lease on the Airton Friends' property was acquired by William and Alice Ellis from the Lambert estate in 1700, for £31. This purchase is commemorated by their initials and the date carved into the lintel under the Meeting House porch. According to the deed of purchase, the property comprised *all that one parcel of arable or meadow land commonly called The Croft containing by estimation half an acre be the same more or less and all that one house, barn or stable situate standing and being on that part of the said parcel of ground which doth adjoyne to the Common Street in the said Ayrton.* Here, as in other records, no overt acknowledgement is made of the function which the Meeting House was built to serve and which it had been serving for most or all of the previous century. A 1951 account of the charitable trusts of Brighouse, Leeds and Settle Monthly Meetings says that the Meeting House, cottage and stable had been leased by William and Alice Ellis from John Lambert, son of the Major-General, in March 1700 for a term of 5,000 years, and given by the Ellises in trust to Friends in 1706, with the intention that any rents which might be obtained from the property should be applied towards repair of the Meeting House and the premises adjoining. The deed of conveyance to trustees speaks of the Meeting House and *the stable for them to put their horses in*, together with a croft of which part was to be for burials and the remainder *for getting of hay on for their horses when they shall meet*. This mention of a stable is somewhat unclear. It may reflect reuse as a stable of the small and by then dilapidated former cottage which Alice Ellis had repaired and enlarged in 1710, or possibly there was another more ephemeral structure which served that purpose. A blocked-off gateway to the hay meadow can be seen in the south perimeter wall of the burial ground. There is, according to Thistlethwaite (1979 pp. 97 and 412), a Yorkshire Quarterly Meeting record of Airton Meeting House dating to 1696, which may be taken as a definite *terminus ante quem*. However, since local meeting houses first began to be recorded in that year it seems to be a record of the existence of the already well established Airton Meeting House or perhaps a reference to its then recent refurbishment.

Two letters written by William Ellis in 1697 (Backhouse, 1849 pp 29 & 33) are of particular interest. The first of these, from London, is addressed *to Simeon Wilkinson, with the rest of my servants*; in it he urges them to attend midweek Quaker meetings and to *consider why there are so many that fall asleep when met together to worship God.* The second letter, from Airton, has no named addressee and is dated the *24ᵗʰ of the 6ᵗʰ month* 1697, shortly before William sailed to America; it is quoted and discussed chapter eight, above. *I have laboured with my soul, body and substance... to bring Truth up into dominion over all the country where I live.... Many public-Friends come to us, and great numbers of people at times....* From the first of these letters it may be deduced that regular midweek as well as first-day meetings were held in the Meeting House directly across the road from the weaving workshop, as it is improbable that the business could have prospered if those by whom it was staffed had been allowed time to go further afield. Drowsiness at these meetings may have arisen from people who led physically active lives, usually outdoors or in unheated rooms, having an opportunity to sit at ease in a room which may have been heated by a fireplace and chimney. If there was such a feature, it must have been replaced when two new fireplaces and a new chimney were inserted in 1710. In the second letter, he wrote of the improvements he had made to the Meeting House. By then, it was probably well in need of refurbishment. Consideration of events in William's life make it most likely that transformation of the one-roomed Meeting House in which Friends had been meeting for the previous 45 or so years into the two-roomed Meeting House that we know today would have been in about 1693. The style of the oak wainscot panelling, the partition wall with its drop shutters, and their nailed butterfly-shaped hinges all belong to the late seventeenth century. Insertion of the small side window in Airton Meeting House's north face, at the end of the raised bench also dates to the 1690s. Especially before the south-facing windows were enlarged, the extra light provided by this window would have been needed so that senior Friends sitting on the raised bench could read out letters from other Quaker meetings, epistles from Yearly and Quarterly Meetings, Bible passages, etc. By the time of its acquisition from the Lambert estate, the early-seventeenth-century Meeting House had had its raised bench along the west wall, oak partition screen and oak wainscot panelling inserted. These are the alterations to which William Ellis referred.

When the alterations made by William and Alice Ellis were completed, the meeting house would have had a much more sombre appearance than it does now. Traces of the original paint on its lime-plastered walls were discovered when the meeting house was restored in 2007. The main meeting room had been painted a dull ochre yellow-brown. On the walls of the gallery above there was a darker brick red paint. The pigment for these colours could have derived from local sources on Malham Moor. We do not have a certain date for creation of the upstairs gallery in the Meeting House; however, the balance of probabilities is that this was inserted in 1710, when the Meeting House roof was raised to align it with that of newly-rebuilt cottage, The Nook. Some features of Airton's woodwork and layout are duplicated at Farfield Meeting House, which was purpose built in 1697. Rylstone Meeting House, built on The Raikes between Rylstone and Hetton in about 1711 and used for Quaker meetings for worship until 1792, is thought to have had a very similar configuration of rooms, windows, and gallery to that at Airton. Its eighteenth-century fireplace is an almost exact duplicate of that on Airton's gallery. Our Meeting House's configuration of two rooms separated by a wooden screen with hanging shutters, with a fireplace in the smaller room and a gallery overhead became a common one for early Quaker meeting houses. A particularly good example of this layout may be seen in Northumberland at Coanwood Meeting House, which was built in 1760.

Visitors to Airton Meeting House frequently ask what was the function of the small room that is set off by the partition wall and hanging shutters. Particularly in letters written in 1672 and 1673 (Epistles 291 and 296), George Fox advocated women Friends' participation in the administration of Quaker affairs and the establishment of separate women's meetings for church affairs to facilitate this. The first women's Quarterly Meeting in Yorkshire was held in 1677, occasionally thereafter until the early-eighteenth century, then twice or thrice in most years until 1778, thereafter four times a year until the end of 1906. Subsequently, there has been no separation of men's and women's participation in Friends business and administration (Thistlethwaite 1979, p. 23). At the local level, women's meetings were intended to take care of local affairs and to prepare reports and brief delegates to be sent to the women's Quarterly Meetings, usually held in York. The main use of the shuttered, smaller meeting room under the gallery in the Airton Meeting House would have been to give women Friends a convenient place in which to consider such church affairs as most concerned them: the education of children, placing of apprentices, approval of marriages, relief of the poor and the care of orphans, elderly and infirm Friends. After their meetings in the warmth with shutters closed, the shutters could be raised so that they and men Friends holding simultaneous business meetings in the larger room could confer with and report to one another. It may be conjectured that the Airton partition with drop shutters was designed by Alice Ellis, who had a particular interest in fostering women's participation in Quaker church affairs. As far as we are aware, it is the oldest surviving example and may have been the prototype of this distinctive feature of early Quaker meeting houses.

In 1710, the year after William's death, Alice Ellis had the small stable or dwelling on the west end of the Meeting House rebuilt and enlarged to serve as a cottage for a Resident Friend and new stables with a hayloft over [the present Barn] built at right angles to, but not contiguous with, the Meeting House. That the remains of the stone canopy over The Barn's west entrance resembles the canopy over the Meeting House door, corroborates written records that both are of the same age. A no-longer-extant lane then ran past the west front of the new stables. Remodelling of the Meeting House which took place at this time included insertion of two fireplaces and a chimney, enlargement of the windows and probably insertion of the gallery. Dressed stones for the windows and fireplaces may have been ready-made items kept in stock by local masons. The Nook and the Meeting House were reroofed to a common height. The repositioning of oak wainscot panels from the main floor of the Meeting House to serve as facing along the gallery rail probably occurred much later. The extent of whitewash on the walls in the roof void above the main room of the Meeting House implies that its ceiling was formerly higher than it is now. In keeping with Friends' practices of simplicity and reluctance to commemorate individuals, early meeting houses usually have dates without initials, as at Farfield, Skipton and Settle. As discussed above, the date, 1700, marks the acquisition by William and Alice Ellis of the meeting house, not its initial construction.

Two other early Quaker meeting houses in our area, those in Skipton and at Farfield, were purpose-built in the seventeenth century. Each is a vernacular, barn-like structure with symmetric windows and a centrally-placed door on a non-gable side wall; although not as carefully concealed as the Airton Meeting house, they are each inconspicuous in their settings and in their absence of decorative features. The indenture, or deed of purchase, for Farfield Meeting House is dated the sixteenth day of *the month called September*, 1689. That document states that the Farfield building was being erected by the purchasers at the time of its purchase. Skipton Meeting House dates to 1693. Having begun as very similar structures in the seventeenth century, these three meeting houses now display the characters of different stages in their subsequent development. Except for its heightened roof, Farfield Meeting House looks much as it may have done when it was first built. As detailed above, Airton Meeting House largely retains its late-seventeenth- and early-eighteenth-century appearance. Skipton Meeting House has retained some seventeenth-century panelling and a mutilated mid-eighteenth-century partition screen whose design appears to be a more sophisticated version of Airton's. Together, these three buildings constitute an interesting and valuable record of regional vernacular architecture as expressed in Friends meeting houses.

No specific records have been found of alterations made to the Airton buildings during most of the eighteenth and nineteenth centuries, though it is apparent that periods of neglect alternated with occasional changes. In the early- to mid-nineteenth century The Barn was reroofed, its walls raised to provide a full-height first floor, and the building extended northwards to abut the south wall of The Nook. When The Barn was extended, an original door which must have existed in its east wall was replaced by a new entrance in its west face behind the present external stairs to the first floor. The double doors to this new entrance pivoted in wooden sockets, one of which is still visible. Quoin stones framing part of the present main entrance to The Barn on its east side indicate the original south-east corner of the stables. Probably it was during the late-eighteenth or early-nineteenth century that changes were made to the layout of the grounds: a north-south wall delimiting the original stable- or barnyard was reduced to below ground level. In the Meeting House, the pine wainscoting, lower facing-bench and repositioning of oak wainscot panels to front the gallery are late-eighteenth-century features. The relatively recent date of the present ceiling of the Meeting House is unknown. Reused timbers indicate that the Meeting House roof structure has been altered several times. Insertion of an iron fireplace into the ground floor surround, widening of the seat of the pine facing-bench and insertion of the large window in the north wall may date to the late nineteenth century. Repairs and some temporary alterations were made when the Meeting House was prepared to accommodate two war-displaced families from Liverpool. The relatively new, wide-board pine ground floor rests on sleeper walls; it does not cover the remains of any earlier hard flooring. Lack of wear on the stairs leading to the Meeting House gallery indicates that they probably replace an older, similar construction. The wide oak planks of the gallery floor look as if they were salvaged and repurposed from the original floor of the Meeting House.

During all this time, as more recently, administration of the Airton Trust Property by Settle Monthly Meeting was not without its problems. In 1774, York Quarterly meeting instructed *Settle Monthly Meeting to use the necessary means, that the remaining Trustees take care to remove the present Tenant* [of the farmland and associated buildings including Ellis House], *& to consider of a proper addition to the number of Trustees....* (Thistlethwaite, 1979 p.89). In 1784 additional land was purchased to add to the Airton Trust Property to make it attractive for renting to a tenant farmer. Funds held by another charitable trust, in favour of a Friends school in Newton-in-Boland, were invested in the purchase of another freehold property in Airton in 1850 (Thistlethwaite p. 207). It is not clear whether this land was included when, in 1852, the Airton Trust Property's allocation of recently-enclosed common land was sold or when, in 1904, the entirety of the estate was sold, except for the present Airton Friends Property and the Ellis's house and its adjoining Quaker Cottage (now called Ellis Barn), across the road from our Meeting House (Thistlethwaite 1979, pp. 101 and 207). Ellis House and Quaker Cottage were sold in the 1920s.

When Arnold and Phyllis Waterfall moved into The Nook in 1944, they found it in a poor state of repair and needing improvements. Downstairs, they had a solid fuel Aga installed; upstairs, they divided off part of a long narrow bedroom to provide space for a bathroom and incorporated part of the loft of the adjacent Barn to create two further bedrooms. This incorporation was reversed and The Nook restored to its older two-bedroomed plan when The Barn was renovated in 2011. They also had a bitumen-tar coating spread over the kitchen floor in a not-entirely-successful attempt to deal with problems of rising damp. Concerning The Barn, Arnold Waterfall says that *When we arrived, the place hadn't been used for years except as the occasional kipping down place for Young Friends. The floor was full of holes and really unsafe, and the roof leaked in several places....* As discussed above, they were energetic and successful in reversing this situation. When they left Airton in 1965, care of the property and premises was assumed by a committee appointed by Settle Monthly Meeting.

In 1983, the committee partitioned the first floor of The Barn to create three bunkrooms, installed a shower, modernised the kitchen, and made other improvements from time to time. However, when a new committee was appointed in 2002 it was found that all three buildings, the Meeting House, The Nook and The Barn, were in poor states of repair. On the advice of fire-safety and health officers, The Barn, which by then was generating little income from its use as a hostel, was temporarily closed while essential basic improvements were made. In the Meeting House, sodden and filthy floor coverings were removed, no more than three people were allowed onto the ill-supported gallery at a time, and attempts begun to get a tardy builder to complete the structure's reroofing. By the time roof repairs were completed in 2004, the Meeting House had been left partially unroofed for 18 months. It is a matter of pride that the restoration of the Meeting House, which was completed in 2008, did very little to alter its appearance. The most visible items of new work are the light fixtures, the heating system, and a T-loop to assist people who use hearing aids. Traces of lead-based paint remain on the seventeenth-century panelling as these could not be removed without damaging the fragile wood. Unlike the Meeting House, The Barn was in such a poor state that it had to be almost completely gutted; only its upstairs beech floor and the post and rafters supporting its roof could be retained. The original, westward-facing external stone stairs to the first floor were replaced by a stone and metal staircase oriented towards the road. The renovated Barn was reopened in 2011. The almost £300,000 cost of works to The Barn and Meeting House plus repair of the garden wall and shed, and installation of stone paving to replace tarmac around the Meeting House was met by a well-supported fundraising campaign. In addition, the owners of the Airton Trust Property, the Brighouse, Leeds and Settle Monthly Meetings' Joint Buildings Charity paid for repairs to and modernisation of The Nook, which were completed in 2010.

It is perhaps worth recording that the ceiling light globes in the Meeting House and in The Barn and the brass umbrella stands just inside the Meeting House door were purchased from the Airton Methodist Chapel when it closed in 2004. The Meeting House benches with movable backs were also acquired from the Methodist Chapel, probably in the 1950s. Some others of the benches, those that are the most worn and disreputable looking, have been part of the Meeting House furniture at least since the early 1900s, perhaps for much longer. A set of spindle-backed wooden chairs was donated to Airton Meeting by the Kilnsey and Conistone Parish Hall Committee. These were probably locally made in the 1930s. A narrow bench on the Meeting House gallery comes from the Newton-in Boland meeting house; it incorporates a board onto which are carved the initials *J. B.,* thought to be those of the Quaker Politician John Bright (1811 – 1889) who had attended a Quaker school in Newton.

13.   Interments in the Airton Burial Ground

A list of recorded interments in the Airton Meeting House burial ground compiled by David Tippey for the Malhamdale Local History Group forms the basis for the following section. I have reformulated this with some additions and corrections. The absence of burial records predating 1663 does not necessarily preclude its use during the first half of the seventeenth century by Seekers or other Dissenters, who either did not keep formal records of their associates and activities or whose records have not survived. Owing to the post-1660 nominal synoecism that frequently attributed Airton Meeting House, Meeting and burial ground to *Rylstone*, sometimes to *Scale House*, and at least once to Flasby, it is not possible to fully disentangle the earlier Airton and the Rylstone burial records. However, the first recorded burials, of three members of the Wilkinson family, would certainly have taken place in Airton. The Simeon Wilkinson who was a correspondent and a senior employee of William Ellis in 1697 may have been the husband, or perhaps the son of Ann Wilkinson who died in 1668.

Among the more recent interments, no distinction is made in the following list between actual burials and the deposition of cremated ashes, although these are distinguished within the burial ground. Interments of ashes are more closely spaced than are burials and they are situated in the northern part of the grounds, in the area which was the first to be used as a burial plot. Starting in the last quarter of the nineteenth century, several members of the interrelated Waterfall and Cartwright families were interred in Airton. When Waterfalls moved away from Malhamdale, it seems to have been a family custom to return their ashes to Airton for burial. Some irregularities occurred towards the end of the twentieth century, when little oversight was exercised over how the Meeting House and grounds were used. The ashes of George Camm, husband of Ruth Camm, were interred without any Quaker record being made or permission obtained. George and Ruth were members of Skipton Quaker Meeting. Even more unusually, a memorial commemorating Richard Arthur Bedford-Payne (1928 – 1994), a member of Skipton Meeting and husband of Brontë, was erected in the Airton Burial ground, although neither his body nor his ashes are buried here. Subsequently, this large engraved stone, for which permission had neither been sought nor granted, was removed from its prominent position and, in 2018, incorporated into a new stone bench. As of 2009, a policy was agreed that restricts use of the Airton Meeting House burial ground to people closely connected to Airton Local Meeting or, for the interment of ashes, to Craven and Keighley Area Meeting. The 126 names listed here may not be a complete record of all whose bodies or ashes are interred in the Airton Meeting House burial ground and some who are listed, particularly among the Waterfall family members, may have had only a tenuous connection with Malhamdale and with Airton Quaker Meeting. Similarly, particularly in the earlier years there may have been some interments that are not entered in Quaker records. However, it may be assumed that all who are listed were members of Quaker families. It is noteworthy that seven family names account for almost half of the entries on this list: Wilkinson, Anderson, Squire, Parkinson, Shakleton, Waterfall, and Cartwright.

Looking at the frequency of interments gives an approximate indicator of the relative size of Airton Meeting at different periods. Between 1663 and 1795 there was approximately one-and-a-half years between burials. It was during this period that William Ellis wrote of *great meetings* being held at Airton and of his hopes that all of Malhamdale would become Quakers, and during which Alice Ellis had a large new stable and hayloft built to accommodate the horses of people who came to Quaker meetings in Airton. It may perhaps be wondered why in the period between about 1660 and 1720 there were not more burials at Airton. Several reasons can be suggested for this. Perhaps most cogent is that in the seventeenth century Quakerism was a notably youthful religion; many people joined Friends as young adults, as did John Hall and William Ellis. Consequently, there would have been relatively few Quaker deaths from old age before about 1710. Then as now, opportunities to earn a living in the Yorkshire Dales were not as plentiful as in urban areas. By the time they were elderly, some of the younger members of Malhamdale Quaker families and some entire families would have moved to towns and cities where they hoped to prosper and some would have emigrated abroad. An equally significant reason is implied by the new stable and hayloft. The Meeting House was the largest indoor space available to local Friends during most of the seventeenth century. It was the place where prominent visiting Quakers would come to worship and to preach and more than a few Friends might travel long distances to hear them. Probably they were joined by others who did not usually worship with Friends, but who were interested in religious issues and in hearing what a Quaker preacher had to say. Such people would eventually be interred nearer to their own homes and in the burial grounds of the churches to which they were affiliated, not in Airton.

The following period, from 1807 to 1877 was one of urban development, emigration and rural decline. This trend is reflected in the Airton burials, which decreased to an average rate of approximately one every six years. When Dewhurst developed its cotton-spinning mill in Airton in the last decades of the nineteenth century, the population of Malhamdale, and especially of Airton, increased. It was during this time that the Airton Meeting House is said to have sometimes accommodated as many as 200 people and the Methodist chapel to have welcomed even larger congregations. It was also during this period that an Adult School was started in the Meeting House. This increased activity is reflected in an average burial rate of one every two years between 1882 and 1912. There were no recorded burials between 1912 and 1921. In the subsequent period, from 1921 to 1994, the average rate of interment was one every eight years, with some of these being the deposition of imported ashes. Between 2003 and 2018, there have been five interments plus the scattering of ashes of Malcolm Whalan (18 April 1945 – 8 November 2016, of Devon Area Meeting) in 2018, and of Margaret Knight (25 June 1934 – 19 August 2018 of Exmouth Meeting), giving an average rate of approximately one every two-and-a-half years. Malcolm was formerly very active among Yorkshire Friends, and was the very supportive Clerk of the Brighouse, Leeds and Settle Monthly Meetings' Buildings Charity during most of the period when plans were made and funds raised for the restoration of the Airton Trust Property. Margaret, who had formerly lived in Threshfield, intended to join Friends worshipping in Airton. Sadly, she was unable to do so as she was severely incapacitated soon after her return to Threshfield. As theirs were not interments, Malcolm and Margaret are not included in the following list.

1661 – 1680
Isabell Wilkinson, of Knowlebank, died 7 February 1663
Thomas Wilkinson, son of Isabell, died 14 My 1668
Ann Wilkinson, wife of Simeon, died 22 September 1668
Abraham Binds/Binns, of Kirkgillhouse, died 12 December 1669
William Wigglesworth, of Gargrave, died 12 March 1669
Elizabeth Wainman, wife of William, died 27 April 1669
Stephen Kitching, of Fleits, died 14 November 1669
Alice Squire, of Airton, died 19 March 1675

Sarah Wilkinson, sister of Simeon, died 12 November 1675
Ellin Thompson, died 4 January 1680
Thomas Anderson, of Hanlith, died 6 February 1680

1681 – 1700

Thomas Preston, of Airton, died 12 December 1681
Elizabeth Preston, wife of Thomas, died 16 June 1681
John Squire, son of John, died 20 November 1682
Mary Squire, died 2 February 1683
John Squire, son of John, died 27 May 1685
Martha Stowe, of Winterburn, died 17 January 1693
John Squire, Son of Thomas, died 18 June 1695
Ambrose Smith, died 24 April 1696
Grace Wainman, wife of William, died 29 November 1700

1701 – 1720

Thomas Atkinson, of Malham, died 23 January 1706
John Shackleton, of Airton, died 21 June 1706
William Smith, son of John of Leeyeat, died 30 June 1706
John Smith, son of John of Leeyeat, died 1 August 1706
Jane Anderson, wife of William of Malham, died 29 April 1707
Phineas Parkinson, of Bell Busk, died 1 May 1708
Isabel Parkinson, wife of Phineas, died 18 May 1708
Jane Parkinson, wife of Simeon, died 30 August 1709
Robert Parkinson, son of Simeon, died 30 August 1709
William Ellis, master linen weaver of Airton, died 4 June 1709
Henery Gill, of Airton, died 29 September 1712
Richard Wilkinson, of Otterburn, died 7 November 1714
John Tomlinson, of Gargrave, died 28 February 1718
Margaret Squire, wife of Adam, died 5 March 1718
Mary Jarrat, of Otterburn, died 19 November 1719
Mary Squire, daughter of Adam, died 18 June 1720
Alice Ellis, widow of William, died 27 July 1720, aged 57 years
Catherine Geldard, daughter of Thomas and Ann, died 27 July 1720

1721 – 1740

Mary Anderson, daughter of John of Hanlith, died 10 June 1721
Ann Elsay, of Gargrave, died 9 November 1723
John Anderson, of Hanlith, died 24 August, 1727
Sarah Hall, wife of Joseph of Airton, died 4 July 1728
Ann Anderson, wife of John of Malham, died 18 October 1730
Ann Anderson, widow, died 6 April 1731
Margaret Wilkinson, widow, died 5 July 1731, aged 88 years
Adam Squire, of Airton, died 17 September 1733
John Parkinson, of Bell Busk, died 16 February 1735
Mary Carr, of Coniston Cold, widow, died 8 December 1735
Judith Rawson, daughter of John of Airton, died 6 April 1737
Phineas Parkinson, of Gargrave, died 25 July 1738
Martha Rawson, daughter of John, died 26 November 1738
Jennet Taylford, wife of David, died 20 August 1739, aged 79 years

Thomas Audus, son of John of Malham, died 11 April 1739, aged 2 weeks
Simeon Watkins, son of Richard, died 26 April 1740

1741 – 1760
Mary Blakey, wife of William, died 30 March 1741
William Stockdale, died 2 December 1741
Thomas Anderson, of Hanlith, died 6 January 1743
Elizabeth Bradley, wife of Richard of Calton, died 11 August 1744
Margaret Squire, died 16 September 1748
Thomas Geldard, died 9 November 1748
Elizabeth Bulack, wife of David of Airton, died 29 May 1750
William Blakey, of Malham, died 26 March 1753
Edward Veepon, of Airton, died 13 June 1756
Hannah Wilkinson, widow of Simeon, died 26 September 1756
Richard Bradley, of Calton, died 24 March 1758
Thomas Bradley, of Calton, died 13 April 1758
Mary Bradley, of Calton, died 16 April 1758
John Rwson, died 4 December 1758

1761 – 1780
Anna Geldard, widow of Thomas of Airton, died 24 October 1764
Edward Veepon, son of Edward, late of Airton, died 3 June 1770
Hanna Veepon, widow of Edward, horse dealer, late of Airton, died 20 January 1771, aged 61 years
John Squire, of Airton, husbandman, died 20 February 1774 aged 64 years
Martha Shackleton, wife of Joseph, shalloon maker of Calton, died 31 October 1778, aged 56 years [shalloon is a loosely-woven worsted cloth]
Elizabeth Bradley, daughter of Richard & Elizabeth of Calton, died 17 December 1778, aged 54 years
Mary Parkinson, wife of Robert of Gargrave, died 23 June 1779, aged 69 years
Mary Blakey, wife of Samuel, grocer of Gargrave, died 21 July 1779, aged 39 years

1781 – 1800
Mary Hart, daughter of John & Mary of Gargrave, died 24 June 1783, aged 10 months
Phinehas Parkinson, linen bleacher of Gargrave, died 8 October 1784, aged 80 years
Mary Hart, daughter of John & Mary of Gargrave, shop keeper, died 24 June 1785, aged 10 months [NB. same death is also recorded for 1783]
Hannah Clough, daughter of Anthony of Broughton Field, died 22 January 1786, aged 60 years
Ann Stow, widow of Jesse, linen weaver of Airton, died 16 January 1789, aged 99 years
Ralph Hart, son of John & Mary, linen drapers of Gargrave, died 20 July 1789, aged 1 year
Martha Squire, widow of John of Airton, died 12 March 1790, aged 88 years
Joseph Shackleton, farmer of Calton, died 23 April 1790, aged 67 years
Sarah Parkinson, widow of Phineas of Gargrave, died 9 May 1794, aged 77 years
David Stow, linen weaver of Airton, died 4 May 1795, aged 79 years

1801 – 1820
Robert Hargraves, worsted spinner, Holme House, Linton, died 9 October 1807, aged 70 years
Deborah Hargraves, widow of Robert of Holme House, died 6 May 1808, aged 72 years

Martha Veepon, spinster of Airton, daughter of Edward & Hannah, died 22 September 1813, aged 70 years

Mary Stow, widow of David, linen weaver of Airton, died 1 May 1817, aged 85 years

1821 – 1840

Martha Wharf, daughter of Thomas & Agnes, died 14 February 1831, aged 6 weeks

Richard Shackleton, son of John & Ann, of Airton, died 4 October 1831, aged 2 weeks

Richard Shakleton, corn dealer of Airton, died 14 October 1831, aged 77 years

1841 – 1860

Mary Coates, died 18 June 1859, aged 81 years

1861 – 1880

Lucy Ann Waterfall, of Kirkby Malham, died 5 May 1874, aged 1 year

Edmund Waterfall, infant son of Arthur of Kirkby Malham, died October 1876

Hannah Maria Waterfall, wife of Arthur of Kirkby Malham, died 20 January 1877, aged 34 years

1881 – 1900

George Cartwright, of Airton, died 10 February 1882, aged 79 years

Ann Cartwright, of Airton, died 23 September 1884, aged 80 years

Rachel Cartwright, of Airton, died 5 May 1886, aged 52 years

William Spencer, died 1891 aged 33 years

Arthur Waterfall, of Leeds, died October 1891, aged 57 years

Thomas Braithwaite, of Airton, died 17 May 1896, aged 80 years

Sarah Maria Smith, died 7 September 1896, aged 71 years

Robert Chester, of Skipton, died 30 November 1896, aged 82 years

George H. Waterfall, of Horsforth, died 29 March 1899, aged 32 years

1901 – 1920

George Cyril Waterfall, son of Arthur & Lillian of Halifax, died March 1901, aged 7 months

Richard Shakleton Spencer, died 11 September 1904, aged 79 years

Sarah Ann Cartwright, of Airton, died 10 April 1906, aged 74 years

Mary Cartwright, of Airton, died 5 October 1906, aged 70 years

Elizabeth Cartwright, died 27 May 1909, aged 81 years

Mary Spencer, died 6 October 1912, aged 86 years

1921 – 1940

Martha Egroyd Baines, of Rose Mount, Airton, died 7 July 1921, aged 88 years

Arthur Wilson Waterfall, died 9 April 1931, aged 62 years

1941 – 1960

Edith Waterfall, died 15 October 1945

Lilian Waterfall, died 24 July 1960, aged 87 years

1961 – 1980

Kathleen Green, (formerly Pickles & Waterfall), died 14 February 1965, aged 68 years

Maurice H. Waterfall, died 12 December 1977, aged 65 years

1981 – 2000

Arnold C. Waterfall, resident Warden of Airton Meeting House, died 7 May 1990, aged 76 years

Joseph John Waterfall, died 27 February 1994, aged 69 years

Phyllis Waterfall, resident Warden of Airton Meeting House, died 1 October 1994, aged 81 years

2001 – 2020

George Leslie Camm, died 2000, aged 86 years

E. Phyllis Waterfall, died 8 January 2003, aged 88 years

Ruth Camm, mathematics teacher of Gargrave, wife of George, died 2011, aged 90 years

Kevin Berry, journalist of Scosthrop, died 12 August 2014 aged 68 years

Roger Waterfall, travel agent of Silsden, son of Arnold & Phyllis, died 24 August 2014, aged 70 years

Brontë Bedford-Payne, dentist of Grassington, wife of Richard, died 6 August 2017, aged 88 years

14. Bibliography

Anon., 2006. The Society of Friends. *Times Past, newsletter of the Bordley-Cracoe-Hetton-Rylstone Local History Group.*

Ashley, M., 1954. *Cromwell's Generals.* London: Jonathan Cape.

Backhouse, J., 1849. *The Life and Correspondence of William and Alice Ellis of Airton.* London: Charles Gilpin, and York: John Linney.

Barclay, A. R. 1841. *Letters, &c., of Early Friends; illustrative of the History of the Society, from nearly its origin, to about the period of George Fox's decease...* London: Harvey and Darton.

Barker, P.& E. Vernon [eds.], 2012. *The Agreements of the People, the Levellers and the Constitutional Crisis of the English Revolution.* Basingstoke: Palgrave Macmillan.

Baumber, M. L., no date [*circa* 1975]. *A Pennine Community on the Eve of the Industrial Revolution, Keighley and Haworth between 1660 and 1740.* Keighley: published by the Author.

Benn, T., 2000. *The Levellers and the English Democratic Tradition.* Nottingham: Spokesman Books.

Besse, J., 1753. *A collection of the Sufferings of the People Called Quakers, taken from Original Records and Authentick Accounts.* 1998 facsimile reprint of the Yorkshire entries. York: Sessions Book Trust.

Booth, C., 2005. The Quakers of Countersett and their Legacy, *Journal of the Friends Historical Society.* 60, 3: 157-179.

Boulton, D., 2002. *Real Like the Daisies or Real Like I Love You: essays in radical Quakerism.* Hobsons Farm, Dent: Dales Historical Monographs.

Butlin, R. A., 2003, *Historical Atlas of North Yorkshire.* Otley, Westbury Publishing.

Boulton, D., & A. Boulton, 1998. *In Fox's Footsteps.* Hobsons Farm, Dent: Dales Historical Monographs.

Brailsford, H. N., edited by C. Hill, 1983 2nd edition [1961 1st edition]. *The Levellers and the English Revolution.* Nottingham: Spokesman.

Brayshaw, T., & W. Oliver (eds) 1938. *The Parish Register of Kirkby Malham in the County of York, vol. I 1597-1690.* Yorkshire Parish Register Society.

Brighouse, Leeds and Settle Monthly Meetings, 1951. *An Account of the Charitable Trusts and Other Properties.* York: William Sessions.

Carroll, W., 2003 [issued 2005]. William Edmundson: Ireland's first Quaker, *Journal of the Friends Historical Society.* 60, 1: 25-35.

Como, D. R., 2004. *Blown by the Spirit, Puritanism and the Emergence of an Antinomian Underground in Pre-Civil-War England.* Stamford, California: Stamford University Press.

Dawson, W. H., 1882. *History of Skipton.* London: Simpkin, Marshall, and Skipton: Edmondson.

Dawson, W.H., 1938. *Cromwell's Understudy, the Life and Times of General John Lambert and the Rise and Fall of the Protestants.* London, Edinburgh & Glasgow: William Hodge.-

Dayes, E., 1805. *The Works of the Late Edward Dayes; and Excursion through the Principal Parts of Derbyshire and Yorkshire.* published by Mrs Dayes.

Diaper, H. (ed.) 2009. *Letters from Malham: Wartime Life at High Barn Cottage.* Leeds: Stanley & Audrey Burton Gallery, University of Leeds.

Evans, W., & T. Evans, 1854. *Piety Promoted in a Collection of Dying Sayings of many of the People Called Quakers, with a brief Account of some of their Labours in the Gospel and Sufferings for the Same.* Philadelphia: Friends Books Store.

Farr, D., 1999. John Blackwell and Daniel Cox: Further Notes on Their Activities in Restoration England and British North America, *Pennsylvania Magazine of History and Biography.* 123, 3: 227-233.

Farr, D. N., 2000. The shaping of John Lambert's allegiance and the outbreak of the Civil War, *Northern History.* 36,2: 247-266.

Farr, D. N., 2003. *John Lambert, Parliamentary Soldier and Cromwellian Major-General, 1619-1684.* Woodbridge, Suffolk: Boydell Press.

Foulds, E. V., 1987 [1952 1st edition]. *The Birthplace of Quakerism, a handbook for the 1652 country.* London: Quaker Home Service.

Gardner, S. R., 1899. *The Constitutional Documents of the Puritan Revolution, 1625-1660.* Oxford: Clarendon Press.

Gomersall, W.J., 1914. *Airton in Malhamdale and other Local Contributions in Prose and Verse: reprints from the Craven Herald.*

Gwyn, D., 2003 [issued 2005]. John Saltmarsh: Quaker Forerunner, *Journal of the Friends Historical Society.* 60, 1: 3-24.

Hall, D., 1758. *Some Brief Memoirs of the Life of David Hall, with an Account of the Life of his Father, John Hall.* London: Luke Hinde.

80

Hall, D. J., 2010. Spreading Friends Books for Truths Service: the distribution of Quaker printed literature in the eighteenth century, *Journal of the Friends Historical Society*. 62, 1: 3-24.

Harland, R., 1993. *The Living Stones of Skipton Quaker Meeting*. Skipton: Skipton Preparative Meeting of the Religious Society of Friends.

Harland, R. & L. Phillipson, 2007. *The Quaker Meeting House at Airton, and some of the Friends who worshipped there*. Airton: Airton Trust Property Management Committee.

Hartley, M., & J. Ingilby, 1956. *The Yorkshire Dales*. republished 1991. Otley: Smith Settle.

Hessayon, A., 2005. Jacob Boehme and the early Quakers, *Journal of the Friends Historical Society*. 60, 3: 191-223,

Hill, C., 1958. *Oliver Cromwell 1658-1958*. London: Routledge and Kegan Paul for the Historical Association.

Holorenshaw, H. [pseud. of J. Needham], 1939. *The Levellers and the English Revolution*. London: Victor Gollancz.

Jennings, B., & The Pateley Bridge Tutorial Class, 1967. *A History of Nidderdale*. Huddersfield: Advertiser Press.

Johnson, D. S., 2018. *Thorns through Time, The story of an abandoned settlement*. Clapham: Yorkshire Dales Millennium Trust.

Jones, R. M., 1914. *Spiritual Reformers in the 16th and 17th Centuries*. London; Macmillan and Co.

Leeds University Library, Special Collections Department, Carlton Hill Archives.

Long, M. H., & M. F. Pickles, 1998. *The Society of Friends in Mid-Wharfedale and Craven 1650-1790*. Ilkley: Mid-Wharfedale Local History Research Group.

Loughlin, S., 2016. *Insurrection, Henry VIII, Thomas Cromwell and the Pilgrimage of Grace*. Stroud: History Press.

Lowther, G., 2003 [issued 2005]. Review of *Seekers Found: Atonement in Early Quaker Experience* by Douglas Gwyn, *Journal of the Friends Historical Society*. 60, 1: 55-8.

Lunnon, C., 2019. *Crisis in the Early 14th Century, a North Yorkshire Local Case Study*. published by the author with the assistance of the Upper Wharfedale Heritage Group.

Martlew, R. D., 2011. Late Prehistory and the Roman Iron Age in Upper Wharfedale: problems, potential and progress. *Prehistory in the Yorkshire Dales, recent research and future prospects,* edited by R. D. Martlew. PLACE, Yorkshire Dales Landscape Research Trust, and Yorkshire Dales National Park Authority

More, T., 1965 [1516 1st edition]. *Utopia.* Harmondsworth: Penguin Books.

Naphy, W., & A. Spicer, 2004. *Plague, Black Death and Pestilence in Europe.* Stroud: Tempus Publishing.

Phillips, C. E. Lucas, 1938. *Cromwell's Captains.* London: William Heineman Ltd.

Phillipson. L., 1988. Quakerism in Cambridge before the Act of Toleration (1653-1689), *Proceedings of the Cambridge Antiquarian Societ.* 77: 1-25.

Phillipson, L., 1998. *The Wisbech Quakers' Roll of 1723.* Cambridge: Cambridgeshire County Council Resources Unit.

Phillipson, L., & A. Armstrong, 2017. *Hidden in Plain Sight, History and Architecture of the Airton Meeting House.* York: Quacks Books.

Pickering, O., 2017. *Josiah Collier of Yeadon (1595 – 1677), West Riding Grindletonian and Disciple of Roger Brearley.* York: University of York Borthwick Institute (Borthwick Paper 127).

Morkill, J. W., 1933. *The Parish of Kirkby Malhamdale in the West Riding of Yorkshire.* Gloucester: John Bellows.

Punshon, J., 2004 [issued 2005]. The Significance of the Tradition: reflections on the writing of Quaker history, *Journal of the Friends Historical Society.* 60, 2: 77-96.

Reckitt, B. N., 1965. *The History of Reckitt and Sons Limited.* London: A. Brown and Sons.

Rooksby, D. A., 1994. *The Quakers in North-west England I, The man in leather breeches.* Eglwysbach, Colwyn Bay: D. A. Rooksby.

Rooksby, D. A., 1998. *The Quakers in North-west England III, And sometime upon the hills.* Eglwysbach, Colwyn Bay: D. A. Rooksby.

Rubinstein, D., 2005. *Yorkshire Friends in Historical Perspective, an Introduction.* York: Quacks Books.

Saltmarsh, J., 1645. *Dawnings of Light, Wherein the True Interest of Reformation is Opened....* London: G. Calvert.

Saltmarsh, J., 1646. *The Smoke in the Temple, Wherein is a Design for Peace and Reconciliation of Believers of the Several Opinions of these Times....* London: G. Calvert.

Sewel, W., 1811 5th edition [1722 1st English edition]. *The History of the Rise, Increase and Progress of the Christian People Called Quakers.* London: William Phillips.

Sharp, W., 1990. *A History of Airton Mill.* Skipton: published by the Author.

Shuffrey, W. A., 1903. *Some Craven Worthies.* London & Leeds: F. E. Robinson, & Richard Jackson.

Smith, W.E. (ed.), 1881. *Old Yorkshire* vol. I, London: Longmans, Green.

Spence, M., 2013. Interpretations of Fourteenth-Century Malham from Documentary Sources. in R. D. Martlew, ed. *Medieval Studies in the Yorkshire Dales.* PLACE/Yorkshire Dales Landscape Research Trust.

Spence, V., 2010. From Late Medieval Piety to Religious Conformity in a Northern Parish: Kirkby Malhamdale, Craven, 1454-1603, *Northern History.* 47, 1: 67-96.

Spence, V., 2012. Early Puritan Evangelism in the North: Christopher Shute, Preacher, Puritan and Vicar of Giggleswick in Craven, 1576 to 1626, *Northern History.* 49, 2: 224-250.

Spence, V., 2015. The Ancient Chapel of St Helen, Malham in Craven: Dissolution and Discovery, *Northern History.* 52, 1: 52-67.

Spence, V., 2016. Adapting to the Elizabethan Settlement: Religious Faith and the Drive Towards Conformity in Craven, 1559 to 1579, *Northern History.* 53, 2: 190-219.

Spence, V., 2017a. Reluctant Reformation in the North: Craven 1547 – 1553, *Yorkshire Archaeological Journal.* 89, 1: 114-133.

Spence, V., 2017b. Craven and the Elizabethan Settlement: Diverging Confessional Identities, 1580 – 1603, *Northern History.* 54, 1: 28-58.

Taylor, E. E., 1942. The Quaker Movement in the Northern Dales, *The Yorkshire Dalesman.* 4,3.

Thistlethwaite, W. P., 1979. *Yorkshire Quarterly Meeting of the Religious Society of Friends, 1665-1966.* Harrogate: published by the author.

Wakeling, C., 2017. *Chapels of England, Buildings of Protestant Nonconformity.* Swindon: Historic England.

Waterfall, A., n.d. *Memoirs.* unpublished manuscript owned by J. Waterfall; A copy is in the archives of the Malhamdale Local History Group.

Whitaker, T. D., 1878 3rd edition [1805 1st edition]. *The History and Antiquities of the Deanery of Craven.* republished in two vols. 1973. Manchester: E. J. Morten, & Skipton: Craven Herald.

Whyte, I. & H. Shaw, 2013. Post-medieval vegetation and landscape change in Upper Ribblesdale: resilience and stability in farming. in R. D. Martlew, ed. *Medieval Studies in the Yorkshire Dales, aspects of history, archaeology and landscape.* PLACE/Yorkshire Dales Landscape Research Trust.

Wilson, K., 1972. *History of Lothersdale.* Lothersdale Parish Council.

Wolf, F. O., 2000. *The International Significance of the Levellers.* Nottingham: Spokesman Books.

Wright, S., 2006. Town and Country: Living as a Friend in Urban and Rural Yorkshire 1780-1860, *Journal of the Friends Historical Society.* 61, 1: 3-31.

York Quarterly Meeting, 1710. *A Brief account of the Life and Death and Some of the Gospel Labours of that Faithful Servant and Minister of JESUS Christ William Ellis.* London: J. Sowle.